An Autosegmental Approach to Shilluk Phonology

Summer Institute of Linguistics and
The University of Texas at Arlington
Publications in Linguistics

Publication 103

Editors

Donald A. Burquest
University of Texas
at Arlington

William R. Merrifield
Summer Institute of
Linguistics

Assistant Editors

Rhonda L. Hartell

Marilyn A. Mayers

Consulting Editors

Doris A. Bartholomew
Pamela M. Bendor-Samuel
Desmond C. Derbyshire
Robert A. Dooley
Jerold A. Edmondson

Austin Hale
Robert E. Longacre
Eugene E. Loos
Kenneth L. Pike
Viola G. Waterhouse

An Autosegmental Approach to Shilluk Phonology

Leoma G. Gilley

A Publication of
The Summer Institute of Linguistics
and
The University of Texas at Arlington
1992

© 1992 by the Summer Institute of Linguistics, Inc.

Library of Congress Catalog No: 91–67484

ISBN: 0–88312–106–9

ISSN: 1040–0850

All Rights Reserved

No part of this publication may be reproduced, stored in a retrieval system, or transmitted in any form or by any means—electronic, mechanical, photocopy, recording, or otherwise—without the express permission of the Summer Institute of Linguistics, with the exception of brief excerpts in journal articles or reviews.

Cover art by Santino Ocay
Cover design by Hazel Shorey

Copies of this and other publications of the Summer Institute of Linguistics may be obtained from

International Academic Bookstore
7500 W. Camp Wisdom Road
Dallas, TX 75236

Contents

Abbreviations and Symbols vii

Preface ix

Acknowledgments x

1. Introduction 1
    1.1 Phonemics 3
    1.2 Generative phonology 4
    1.3 Lexical phonology 5
    1.4 Nonlinear phonology 9
    1.5 Underspecification theory 15
    1.6 Overview 18

2. Phonetics, Phonemics, and Postlexical Phonology 19
    2.1 Phonetic inventory 21
    2.2 Classificatory features 29
    2.3 Redundancy rules 32
    2.4 Nonlinear analysis 35
    2.5 Phonetic tone 44
    2.6 Interpretation of tone 47
    2.7 Underspecification and tone 59
    2.8 Principles of association 60
    2.9 Conclusion 61

vi   Contents

3. Representation of Lexical Items 63
   3.1 Syntax 63
   3.2 Lexical items 81
   3.3 Underlying representation 92

4. Shilluk Syllable Structure 99
   4.1 Surface overview 99
   4.2 Syllable structure tier 100
   4.3 Syllable template 102
   4.4 Restrictions and constraints 104
   4.5 Application of syllable structure 109
   4.6 Plural forms 123
   4.7 Verbs and syllable structure 137
   4.8 Morphology 145
   4.9 Summary 146

5. Lexical Levels of Derivation 153
   5.1 Tone 153
   5.2 Harmony systems 173
   5.3 Inflected singular nouns 182
   5.4 Summary of levels and rules 185

6 Summary and Conclusions 189
   6.1 Advantages of generative phonology 189
   6.2 Independent underlying representations 189
   6.3 Implications for language learning 190
   6.4 Syllable structure 191
   6.5 Composition of Shilluk words 191
   6.6 Features and feature assignments 192
   6.7 The lexicon 192
   6.8 Postlexical level 200
   6.9 Further research 202

References 205

Abbreviations and Symbols

A	Agent	IL	Invariably Long Vowel
AC	Associating Conventions	INDEF	Indefinite
ACT	Active Voice	INFL	Inflection
A/API	Apical	INST	Instrument Marker
APP	Applicative	INTR	Intransitive
ASL	Alternatingly Short and Long Vowels	IS	Invariably Short Vowel
		LAB	Labial
ATR	Advanced Tongue Root	LO	Low
BEC	Bracket Erasure Convention	LOC	Location
BEN	Benefactive	LT	Laryngeal Tier
BENM	Benefactive Marker	MAP	Mapping
BK	Back	N	Noun
C/CNS	Consonant	N-CM	Non-Complement
C-OB	Obligatory Complement	NAS	Nasal
C-OPT	Optional Complement	NIV	New International Version
CCL	Central Closure	NM	Number Suffix, Marker
CM	Complement Marker	NP	Noun Phrase
CMP	Complement	NS	Noun Set
CO	Coda	NUC	Nucleus
COLL	Collective	ONS	Onset
COR	Coronal	OCC	Occlusive
CR	Complement Rule	OCP	Obligatory Contour Principle
DF	Distinctive Feature	P	Patient
DR	Default Rule	PAL	Palatal
[EX]	Expanded Pharynx	PAS	Passive Voice
[F]	Feature	PFX	Prefix
FBU	Feature Bearing Unit	PL	Plural
H, M, L	High, Mid, Low Tone	PS	Possession Marker
HAB	Habitual	PSD	Possessed
HI	High	PSR	Possessor
!H	Downstepped High	PST	Past tense
IIP	I-Incorporation Process	QUAL	Qualitative

vii

Abbreviations and Symbols

RD	Referential Determiner	TA	Tone Assignment
REFL	Reflexive	TBU	Tone Bearing Unit
RESYLL	Resyllabification	TNS	Tense
RM	Rime	V	Vowel
R	Rare	VB	Verb
RND	Round	[VF]	Vowel Features
RT	Root	VIB	Vibrant
S	Subject	VOC	Vocalic
SD	Structural Description	VOI	Voice
SF	Surface Form	UR	Underlying Representation
SFX	Suffix	WD	Word
SG	Singular	WFC	Well-formedness Condition
SGLT	Singulative	x	any filler
SIL	Summer Institute of Linguistics	x'	Unsyllabified X slot
SLT	Supralaryngeal Tier	μ	Morpheme
SON	Sonorant	φ	Phonological
SPE	Sound Pattern of English	θ	Stem
SPG	Spread Glottis	σ	Syllable head
SPRD	Spreading	ω	Word boundary
ST	Stem	1s	First person singular
SVCM	Subject, Verb, Complement	1p	First person plural
SYLL	Syllabification	3p	Third person plural
T	Tone	3s	Third person singular

Preface

Shilluk is a Western Nilotic language spoken in southern Sudan. Previous works on this language have failed to adequately capture the phonological and morphological systems of the language. An Autosegmental approach employed within a framework based upon the tenets of Lexical Phonology, allows the various aspects of Shilluk phonology to be separated in an insightful way. Thus, the vowel and consonant harmony systems, the tonal system, and the syllable structure may be dealt with independently. The volume comprises six chapters: 1. Introduction, 2. Phonetics and Phonology, 3. Representation of Lexical Items, 4. Syllable Structure, 5. Lexical Levels of Derivation, and 6. Summary.

Chapter 2 provides a relatively autonomous account of the consonants, vowels (including length), and tone. Chapter 3 presents evidence for the claim that it is necessary to set up independent underlying representations for the stems of singular and plural nouns, as well as for transitive verb forms. Issues covered in this chapter are tone and the harmony systems—vowel harmony, vowel and consonant harmony, and consonant harmony. Chapter 4 completes the argument for independent representations with a discussion of syllable structure. This chapter shows how syllable structure constraints may be invoked to account for surface vowel length alternations. In turn, this chapter adds another argument for the claim that most lexical items require dual (independent) underlying representations. The material in this chapter demonstrates that processes motivated by syllable structure make it the most influential factor in Shilluk phonology. In chapter 5, the discussion turns to the ordering of levels within the Lexicon. By combining all the tone and syllable structure rules, it is possible to establish the presence of three levels within the Lexicon. A summary of all the rules developed in the volume are given in the sixth chapter along with comments on the implications of this study with regard to language acquisition. Some suggestions are also made for further study.

Special thanks go to the Shilluk community for their patient and willing help in providing the data in this book, and to Dick Hayward for the many hours he put in to help me make sense of the data I had. Thanks also go to Constance Kutsch Lojenga, Gerrit Dimmendaal, and John Harris for the suggestions, constructive criticisms, and encouragement. I have tried to implement many of their improvements in the current version. Any errors which remain are solely my own. Thanks also go to Lorna Priest and Laurie Nelson for conquering the innumerable difficulties of typesetting this work.

This book is dedicated to my parents, without whose love and encouragement it would not have been possible.

1

Introduction

The Shilluk language is spoken by an estimated one-half million people in southern Sudan. The people call themselves *cɔ̀llɔ̀* and the language *ɖɔ́cɔ̀llɔ̀*. The word SHILLUK is an Arabic version of *cɔ̀llɔ̀*.

Shilluk is a Nilotic language. A recent classification by Persson (1984) has categorized Nilotic as in (1).

(1)   Chari Nile
      Eastern Sudanic
         Nilotic Languages
            Northern Nilotic
               North-western Group
                  Lwoian languages
                     Lwo group
                        Northern Lwo sub-group
                           Shilluk

Other languages in the Northern Lwo sub-group include Jur Luwo, Belanda Bor, Shatt (or Thuri), Anuak, and Lokoro (or Pari).

The Shilluk consider their borders to extend from Renk in the north to Tonga in the west to Doleib Hill in the south east. Their villages are concentrated along the Nile River in the vicinity of Malakal.

There are two major Shilluk dialects spoken: *gar* in the north and *lwak* in the south around Doleib Hill. The PUREST Shilluk is said to be spoken around Pachoda where the 'king' (*rɑ̀ṯ*) and his court are located. The data in this book have been collected from individuals originally from the area near Pachoda.

1

Introduction

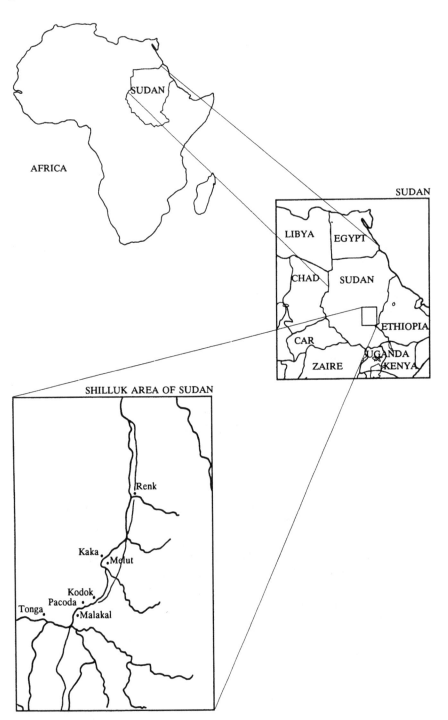

Shilluk Phonology

Shilluk has been the subject of documented linguistic investigation since the early 1900s. Westermann (1912) described the sounds of the language in some detail. He included descriptions of syntactic aspects of the language. In his book there are also a large number of texts with English translations which range over a wide variety of topics.

Kohnen (1933), after some thirty years of study, published his *Shilluk Grammar*. The aim of that work was to facilitate language learning for foreigners. Kohnen followed the orthographic suggestions of the Rejaf Conference (1928) and made no attempt to describe the phonology other than to give a pronunciation guide.

In 1937, Heasty published his *English-Shilluk, Shilluk-English Dictionary*. Again, no analysis was attempted. However, he did include reference to features of vowel length and breathiness in the pronunciation section, although neither length nor breathiness is reflected in the orthography.

Tucker (1955) compiled a paper on the verbs of Shilluk. Both vowel length and breathiness are indicated in the data described. A further work by Tucker and Bryan (1966) compared the various Nilotic languages in east Africa. The information contained is of a descriptive rather than an historical comparative nature.

These works have described various aspects of the Shilluk language in some detail. None of them, however, has attempted to analyze the phonology. My goal in this study is to attempt to do just that.

To accomplish this goal, I have used a primarily nonlinear approach in conjunction with lexical phonology as developed by Kiparsky (1982) and Mohanan (1982), but have also used a somewhat eclectic approach to take advantage of the strengths of certain other models as well, specifically phonemics, generative phonology, nonlinear and lexical phonology, as well as the theory of underspecification. Each of these approaches adds a different facet of insight to our understanding of the hitherto unanalyzed phonology of Shilluk.

1.1. Phonemics

Since Shilluk phonology has not been formally analyzed, it is not possible to come to it with *a priori* assumptions. I begin with the raw phonetic data. Phonemics provides a technique for processing this phonetic data and discovering certain facts about the pertinent units of sound (Pike 1947). According to Pike, the goal is for the outsider to arrive at an analysis which mirrors the perceptions of a native speaker.

One of the practical outworkings of phonemics is the development of an orthography. According to Pike, sounds which are phonemically distinct are

4   Introduction

more easily distinguished by the native speakers than predictable phonetic
variants of a phoneme.

Several orthographies have been devised for Shilluk using the basic
premises of phonemics. The fact that the Shilluks themselves have not
been very successful in learning to read and write with any of these
suggests that the autonomous phoneme might not be an adequate analyti-
cal unit in this language.

An illustration of one of the problems, that of contrastive vowel length
can be seen from (2)–(5).

(2)   [gɔ̄l]   'large hooks'   [gɔ̄l:é]   'his large hooks'
(3)   [gɔ̀:l]   'wild dogs'   [gɔ̄l:é]   'his wild dogs'
(4)   [wát]   'son'   [wá̤:dē]   'his son'
(5)   [wá̤:t]   'sons'   [wá̤t:é]   'his sons'

The issue is complex. An account of vowel length cannot be decided on
the basis of an examination of one form of a word. Lexical and morphosyntactic determinants must be taken into account. This suggests that
an analysis operating with deep, as well as surface, structures might be
more insightful and agree better with the mental categorization of native
speakers. We turn, then, to a generative approach.

1.2. Generative phonology

The usual starting point for generative phonology is the theory presented
in *The Sound Pattern of English* (SPE: Chomsky and Halle, 1968), which
introduces the idea of underlying versus surface representations and a
series of extrinsically ordered rules to derive the latter from the former,
and adopts Jakobson's concept of distinctive features with some modifications. As is pointed out by van der Hulst and Smith (1985:3), there are two
aspects to the theory proposed in SPE: derivational and representational,
both of which have undergone significant changes in recent years. Lexical
phonology has offered changes to the derivational aspect of the theory,
and the various nonlinear approaches have extended its representational
aspect. The more recently developed underspecification theory, moreover,
may be made to function within a nonlinear model. The contribution that
Archangeli (1984) has made to the theory concerns the governed selection
of features which are considered to be present in the classificatory DISTINC-
TIVE FEATURE MATRIX and the massive use of redundancy rules to specify

values in that matrix. We will look in turn at LEXICAL PHONOLOGY, NON-LINEAR PHONOLOGY, and UNDERSPECIFICATION THEORY.

1.3. Lexical phonology

The development of LEXICAL PHONOLOGY grew out of papers by Pesetsky (1979) and Siegel (1974). Pesetsky's analysis of Russian argued that cyclic rules apply in the lexical component after word formation rule applications. Siegel had earlier proposed block or level ordering with phonological rules applying between blocks. Mohanan (1982) and Kiparsky (1982) expanded these ideas into what is now known as lexical phonology.

While the various conceptions of the model differ somewhat, the common idea is to have both "lexical and postlexical applications of phonological rules" (Mohanan 1986:5). LEXICAL PHONOLOGY strives to capture the important relationship between morphology and phonology in terms of a set of levels. I include Mohanan's diagram of the model (1982:11) in (6).

(6)
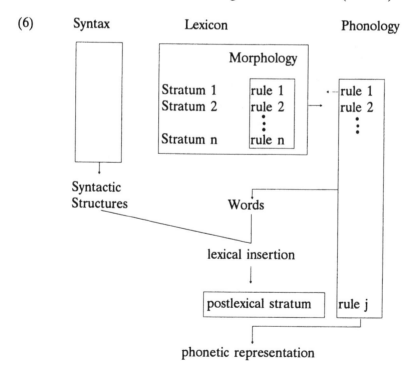

6   Introduction

Within LEXICAL PHONOLOGY, underived lexical items are seen to enter the
first level and are subject to the morphological rules of that level. At the
end of that level, certain lexical phonological rules apply to the structure
if it meets the proper description. The structure then passes through the
next level and follows the same pattern. At the end of the lexical level, the
words are inserted into the syntax where they may undergo postlexical
phonological rules. Postlexical rules have to apply without exception and
have no access to lexical information.

The number of levels and the rules those levels contain seem to be
language specific. English is said to have five morphological domains
including the postlexical level according to Mohanan (1985). Instead of the
'+' or '#' junctural diacritics used in SPE for indicating morphological
levels, the formalism in lexical phonology is restricted to bracketing.
Various levels are shown by the placement of brackets as shown in (7).

(7)   [dis[courage]]

Bracket erasure convention. At each lexical stratum, phonological
rules have access to morphological information. If rules were allowed to
apply cyclically during the lexical derivation, however, the results would
often prove incorrect. In order to restrict cyclic application of rules, BRACK-
ET ERASURE was proposed.

Originally, Chomsky and Halle (SPE 1968) incorporated BRACKET ERASURE
as a part of the definition of cyclic rule application. Later, Pesetsky
suggested that the BRACKET ERASURE CONVENTION (BEC) should be ordered
at the end of every cycle. Mohanan (1982) and Kiparsky (1982) argued
that the BEC should apply only at the end of a lexical stratum. Cole (1987)
presents arguments from English derivational suffixes and from the Seri,
Ci-Ruri, and Sekani languages that rule out the possibility that the BEC
applies cyclically. In her discussion of English, Cole claims that in order to
correctly constrain combinations of suffixes in English, it is necessary to
distinguish derived stems from nonderived ones. If the stratum-final or
cyclic version of the BEC is implemented, then the analysis cannot succeed.

In the case of Seri, /k/ epenthesis occurs in a coronal-m sequence under
two conditions: (i) a morpheme must precede the mood prefix with the
coronal consonant, and (ii) the /m/ must be part of a prefix (Cole
1987:189). In order to meet condition (ii), brackets identifying the root
must be present when /k/-epenthesis applies. If a cyclic application of the
BEC were implemented, root brackets would already have been deleted.
Further, since the root often belongs to a different stratum, even the
stratum-final application of the BEC will eliminate the necessary bracketing
before /k/-epenthesis applies. Cole concludes that "the BEC neither applies

Shilluk Phonology

at the end of every lexical stratum, nor at the end of every cycle" (1987:186). She proposes then, that the BEC may apply once "after all morphological operations have taken place" (1987:203) and further suggests that the formal mechanism which erases brackets is PLANE CONFLATION, which is assumed to occur before the POSTLEXICAL MODULE unless specifically stated otherwise. Thus, all morphological information has been erased by the time the POSTLEXICAL MODULE[1] is reached.

Morpheme planes. Another aspect of LEXICAL PHONOLOGY has to do with the representation of morphemes. Concatenative languages have been traditionally viewed as having strings of morphemes which are either free-standing or bound (i.e., affixes). Nonconcatenative languages such as Arabic, however, do not lend themselves to such a straightforward analysis. In nonconcatenative languages, segments of one morpheme are often interspersed among segments of another morpheme. These morphemes are represented on separate tiers or planes.[2] The identity of a particular morpheme often relates to a canonical pattern (McCarthy 1982:191ff). The canonical pattern tier is referred to by McCarthy as the PROSODIC TEMPLATE. Other sorts of templates are syllables, metrical feet, or even combinations of units from different levels. All tiers are mapped onto the TIMING TIER by means of ASSOCIATION RULES as discussed below in §1.4.

Examples from Sudanese Arabic show four of the possible templates for the root /k t b/ 'write'.

(8)
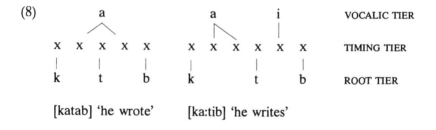

[katab] 'he wrote'   [ka:tib] 'he writes'

---

[1]MODULE is Mohanan's (1986:7) term. It is used synonymously with LEVEL in this study when referring to LEXICAL LEVEL or POSTLEXICAL LEVEL. There are also LEVELS or STRATA within the LEXICAL LEVEL.

[2]PLANE and TIER are considered synonymous in this study.

(9)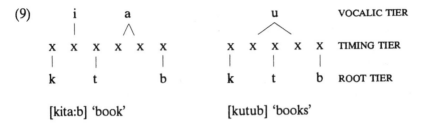

In each case, the root tier is composed of /k/, /t/ and /b/. The vocalic tier, however is interspersed within the root. Since the consonant and vocalic tiers are regarded as independent, either one can be varied apart from the other.

McCarthy (1982:192) suggests that the canonical pattern of morphemes could also be considered a tier in its own right. This tier would specify the number and distribution of the morphemes for a particular form.

Application. From the perspective of LEXICAL PHONOLOGY, then, we see a principled interaction between the morphology and the phonology. Formal acknowledgment of this interaction has helped to resolve some classic problems of analysis in languages like English (Mohanan 1985) and Polish (Rubach 1985; and Booij and Rubach 1987). We will see that certain problems in Shilluk phonology can also be successfully resolved by applying LEXICAL PHONOLOGY.

One fundamental question that arises from the analysis of Shilluk presented here is, What forms are actually derivable? It is generally assumed for most languages that plurals are derived from singulars and that the various verb forms of a single verb paradigm are also derived from a single source, that is, there is an assumption of MORPHEME INVARIANCE. The Shilluk data provide strong evidence that, in this language, two independent representations are needed for each lexical item of the two major categories of NOUNS and VERBS. In other words, independent representations are needed for both singular and plural nouns and for two forms of transitive verbs.

The result of this claim is that twice as much information must be encoded in the LEXICON as has generally been assumed. The resulting expansion in the mechanisms for relating such forms and the memory load required will certainly have implications for our understanding of child language acquisition.

1.4. Nonlinear phonology.

In 1976, Kahn introduced the idea of representing the syllable on a separate tier. He linked syllable nodes to segments by means of association lines of the type used in autosegmental phonology. The value of such a configuration was readily apparent but much debate has been generated over the nature of the structure and representation of it.

Clements and Keyser (1983:7ff) suggest that a third tier be introduced which distinguishes syllable peaks from nonpeaks or margins. He calls this intermediate stage the CV TIER.

(10)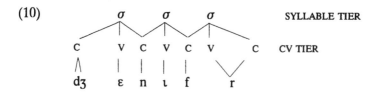

Levin (1983) substitutes x's for c's and v's. Given that the syllable structure defines the nuclear and marginal positions, it is redundant to also specify c and v slots. The c's will fill marginal positions (in most cases) and the v's will fill nuclear slots.

Kurłowicz (1971) proposed that the peak and the coda be grouped into a constituent. He suggested that this grouping is a universal of syllable composition.

Selkirk (1982) divides the syllable into onset and rhyme (or rime). She points out that while there are numerous phonotactic constraints within the onset or within peak and coda, there are no restrictions (at least for English) involving onset and peak. The basic composition of a syllable consists of a template and a set of collocational restrictions. The representation in (11) demonstrates the syllable structure proposed. Selkirk's PEAK will be equated with NUCLEUS in this study.

(11)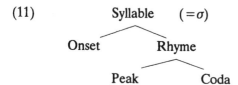

Noske (1982:259) assumes that the onset-rime bipartition is a universal of syllable structure. In addition, he claims that syllabification does not take place at the underlying level. He demonstrates, at least for French, that syllabification applies after at least one phonological rule. Syllabification is also seen to be perseverative (274) so that as the structure changes during the course of the derivation, the syllabification process interacts with that structure to insure that only forms which conform to the syllable template are allowed to surface.

Following McCarthy and Levin, this study assumes that UNDERLYING REPRESENTATIONS are only partially syllabified. Specifically, only the vowel, or syllable head, is indicated. Although in many languages, the syllable headship may be redundant, it is necessary to include it in the underlying representation because Shilluk has both short and long nuclei.

The following notation is used throughout the study: an 'x' represents a timing slot on the timing tier. A syllable head is shown as a vertical line over the appropriate x slot.

The ONSET and CODA of a syllable are filled in during the syllabification process. A syllable head is indicated by *sigma* (σ). A morpheme is shown as *mu* (μ). [F] indicates either a feature or group of features, the specifics of which are not relevant to the discussion.

(12)

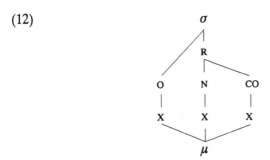

The ONSET and RIME branch first. The RIME may then divide into the NUCLEUS and the CODA.

Delinking of an autosegment is shown as (⟊) and linking as a broken line (......).

(13)   x   x   x   x   x
          | ⟊
         [+F]   [−F]

Shilluk Phonology

Representation. Nonlinear phonology deals with the representational side of generative phonology. In the SPE model, suprasegmental features and segmental features were all placed in the same feature matrix. All were treated equally as segmental features. This solution proved unsatisfactory especially in accounting for tone and vowel harmony.

Goldsmith (1976) argued for a separation of features onto tiers. He suggested a tonal tier which is distinct from, but associated with a segmental tier. That idea was soon applied not only to tone, but to many other phenomena as well.

Poser (1982:126) discussed the features [round] and [back] as autosegments in order to account for vowel and consonant harmony systems of Turkish. He posits the following analysis, for example, for the word *geliyorum* 'I am coming'.

(14)   [−RND] [+RND]   [−RND] [+RND]
          | | ⌐⋯⋯⋯⋯   ⌐⋯⋯⋯⋯
        gel   Iyor   Im → gel   Iyor   Im

                        [geliyorum]

The autosegmentalized feature [round] is attached to the FEATURE BEARING UNIT (a vowel in this case), and allowed to spread until blocked by another occurrence of the same feature, but with an opposite value ([+round], in this case).

Clements and Sezer (1982) also applied a similar autosegmental treatment to harmony in Turkish. They introduced the idea of OPAQUE segments. Opaque segments are lexically assigned and appear, on the surface, to be exceptions to the regular spreading process. The Turkish example in (14) is continued with the rule given by Clements and Sezer (218).

(15)   Roundness Harmony
        P-segments: [+round] [−round]
        Opaque segments: [+syllabic, −high]

Nonhigh vowels are not involved in the roundness system. They are opaque to the roundness harmony. Another example involving opaque segments is found in Laughren (1984) and Kisseberth (1984) where depressor consonants are said to function as opaque elements with regard to tone spreading. These consonants effectively block the further spreading of tone.

12   Introduction

In Vata, there are two sets of vowels. In one set the tongue root is
advanced and in the other it is retracted.

(16)   advanced   retracted

        i   u   ι   ʋ

        e   o   ε   ɔ

                ʌ   a

The harmonic domain is the morpheme. This means that [ATR] harmony
cannot cross a morpheme boundary. All vowels, then, within a given
morpheme must be from the same set.
    Kaye (1982) analyzes the feature [ATR] autosegmentally. The [ATR]
autosegment is shown as [a A]. The representation given by Kaye is shown
in (17).

(17)   retracted   advanced

                            + A   AUTOSEGMENTAL TIER

       gOIU   bIdO   SEGMENTAL TIER

       [gɔlʋ] 'dugout'   [bido] 'wash'

Poser (1982:129) also demonstrated how the feature [nasal] is autosegmentalized to explain the nasal harmony in Guaraní. Voiceless obstruents
are transparent to the harmony. TRANSPARENCY means that a segment does
not participate in a process to either block, trigger or undergo harmony.
Poser explains that the triggers of nasal harmony are the stressed vowels
(both oral and nasal) and nasal stops. These segments are underlyingly
specified for nasality. The remaining segments (targets) receive their nasal
specifications from the triggers.
    Another example of an autosegmental tier comes from Hermans (1985),
who posits separate tiers for laryngeal and supralaryngeal features in his
analysis of preaspiration in Icelandic. The feature [spread glottis] ([SPG])
represents aspiration, for which independent, autosegmental status is argued. The tiers involved, then, are the supralaryngeal (segmental features)
and the laryngeal. Hermans represents aspirated voiceless stops as in (18).

Shilluk Phonology 13

(18)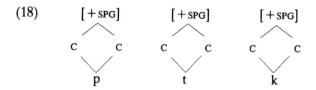

Given this framework, the following DEASPIRATION RULE was proposed for Icelandic, where [+SPG] is delinked from the second half of a geminate cluster.

(19) ICELANDIC DEASPIRATION

[+SPG]
╱╳
C   C

One could go on and on, but the point is that any number of features can be autosegmentalized. With such a wide array of possible autosegments, each with its own tier or plane, it is essential to organize them into a conceptual unit. Clements (1985) suggests two models. The first model is shown as a multitiered structure in which each feature is assigned to its own tier. All the features or tiers are linked to a common core or 'skeleton'. Clements represents the core with c's and v's. Clements' representational geometry (1985:227) is shown in (20).

(20)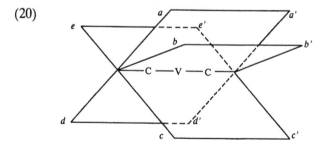

An alternative model, also proposed in Clements' article (1985:229) posits a more complex construction. Again, the CV tier is the core. This model, shown in (21), attempts to capture the componential nature of speech production. Some gestures are more independent than others. Laryngeal configuration, for example, has the highest degree of independence. The degree of nasal cavity stricture, degree and type of oral cavity stricture, and the pairing up of active and passive articulators are cited as showing some degree of mutual independence. One of the values claimed for such a model is that it offers an explanation for assimilation processes.

(21)
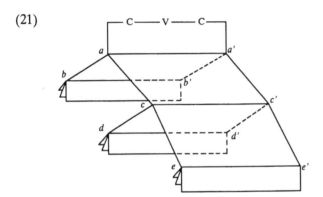

The upper edges represent class tiers: the root tier (*aa'*), laryngeal tier (*bb'*), supralaryngeal tier *(cc')*, manner tier *(dd')*, and place tier *(ee')*. The lower edges are the feature tiers. There could also be a tonal tier.

Cole (1987:18) claims that there is no longer a typological distinction between features involved in spreading or delinking rules in the phonology and those which are not. She argues that the term AUTOSEGMENT is no longer appropriate since all features can be seen as autosegmental. These autosegments can link to or delink from the skeletal tier without reference to any other distinctive feature. The features, then, are seen as independent autosegments. It is here assumed that all features are in principle autosegmental.

In order to define the limits for associating the core with the features or autosegments, Goldsmith (1976) proposed the WELL-FORMEDNESS CONDITION (WFC). A generalized version of the WFC is given in (22). The WFC developed for the autosegmental model applies equally well to the multi-dimensional model described here.

(22) Well-formedness Condition

(a) All FEATURE BEARING UNITS (FBU) are associated to at least one feature.

(b) All features are associated to at least one FBU.

(c) Association lines do not cross.

Shilluk Phonology 15

Some features, such as tone or [ATR], normally attach to a vowel. Other features, such as [labial] or [coronal], usually associate with consonants. In some cases, a feature such as [nasal] may apply to vowels and consonants. It is necessary to define the FEATURE BEARING UNIT (FBU) for each autosegment.

The way in which features are associated with the timing tier was originally proposed by Goldsmith (1976). Haraguchi (1977:331) claimed that only one association line needs to be drawn for language-particular tone rules. All other associations would be made by UNIVERSAL ASSOCIATION CONVENTIONS. A generalized version of Goldsmith's conventions is shown in (23).

(23) Associating Conventions

Mapping: Insert association lines between one feature and one FBU.

Dumping: Leftover features are associated with the nearest FBU.

Spreading: Leftover FBU's are associated with the nearest feature.

Association conventions do not specify where to draw association lines. This decision is language-particular. One of the questions raised by the Shilluk data is, therefore, Where is the first association line drawn? It will be shown that, in Shilluk, the initial association must be made to the ROOT.

1.5. Underspecification theory

One of the principles developed in SPE was that phonological rules operate on fully specified distinctive feature matrices. In contrast to this view, UNDERSPECIFICATION THEORY, as developed by Pulleyblank (1983, 1986) and Archangeli (1984), operates with the premise that there are as few feature specifications in the lexical representation as possible. In order to achieve this goal, two principles are suggested. First, according to the FEATURE MINIMALIZATION PRINCIPLE, one should use the smallest number of distinctive features necessary to keep the phonemes distinct. Secondly, all possible redundancies should be removed from the feature specification.

One means of removing redundancies is to select one value (+ or −) for a particular feature which would be specified in lexical representations. The choice of the value selected is determined by language-specific factors and universal considerations of markedness. The only requirement for underlying phonemes is that they be distinct. It is often the case that one phoneme in each major subsystem (vowels and consonants) may be represented as prosodic functions without any feature specification at all.

16   Introduction

In classical generative phonology, it was assumed that the redundant
feature values which had been omitted from the lexical representation had
to be supplied before any phonological rules were applied. In other words,
the matrices for all segments had to be complete at the beginning of the
phonological component. By contrast, underspecification theory proposes
that redundancy rules apply as late as possible.

If this application of redundancy rules was left unconstrained, a ternary
rather than a binary feature system would result ($+$, $-$, $\emptyset$). The approach
is constrained, however, by the convention that a default rule must assign
[aF] before any rule referring to [aF] in the structural description. Therefore, when a phonological rule refers to a feature that was previously
unspecified, the rules supplying that default value must be ordered prior
to that phonological rule.

There are three types of redundancy rules: DEFAULT rules, COMPLEMENT
rules, and LEARNED rules. DEFAULT rules are context-sensitive and are
assumed to belong to Universal Grammar. A typical example would be:

(24)   [ ] → [−HI] / [___, +LO]

A COMPLEMENT rule supplies the opposite or complementary value to the
one selected for specification in the lexical representation. If, for a particular language, one or more of the vocalic segments were lexically
marked as [−HI], the opposite value would be assigned to the remaining
vocalic segments by means of a complement rule such as (25).

(25)   [ ] → [+HI]

The use of default rules and complement rules is shown below in an
example from the Japanese vowel system. Japanese has five vowels /i e a
o u/ that may be represented by the following matrix.

(26)	i	e	a	o	u
high	−		−		
low		+			
back			+	+	

Shilluk Phonology

The rules needed to complete the matrix are as follows:

(27) $[\ ] \rightarrow [-\text{HI}]/[\underline{\quad},+\text{LO}]$ DR

       $[\ ] \rightarrow [+\text{HI}]$ CR

       $[\ ] \rightarrow [-\text{LO}]$ CR

       $[\ ] \rightarrow [+\text{BK},-\text{RND}]/[\underline{\quad},+\text{LO}]$ DR

       $[\ ] \rightarrow [-\text{BK}]$ CR

       $[\ ] \rightarrow [a\text{RND}]/[\underline{\quad},-\text{LO},\ a\text{BK}]$ DR

If the rules supplied by universal grammar are suspended in some language-specific case, then a LEARNED rule would have to be given. Learned rules would cover a segment that has features such as $[+\text{HI},-\text{BK},+\text{RND}]$. The learned rule would be like the one in (28).

(28) $[\ ] \rightarrow [+\text{RND}] / \underline{\quad\quad\quad}$
$$\begin{bmatrix} -\text{BK} \\ +\text{HI} \end{bmatrix}$$

As mentioned earlier, it is possible to allow one vowel and one consonant to have no feature specifications lexically. This maximally underspecified segment or nonspecified segment is determined solely by the phonological patterns of the language. An epenthetic element is often considered the best candidate for the nonspecified segment. Since that element's function is to make up for deficiencies in the prosodic structure, and since it is not underlyingly present, its feature specification is supplied by rules. If an element is often subject to assimilation, it is a good choice for the nonspecified segment. The ultimate nonspecified segment is the DEFAULT REALIZATION in which all phonic content is supplied by redundancy rules.

One of the advantages of underspecification theory is seen in the process of assimilation. If all features are specified, then the assimilation process involves changing features, as in (29), where the $[-a\text{F}]$ must be delinked from the timing tier. If, however, some features are left unspecified until the end of the derivation, then, using underspecification theory, the process merely fills in a blank matrix, as in (30) where features simply spread to an x slot which is not associated with any feature content. Thus, we see that underspecification theory demonstrates the close relationship between the way segments are used in the phonological system and the underlying matrix and redundancy rules (Archangeli, 1984:60).

(29)   (30)

$$
\begin{array}{cc}
\text{X} & \text{X} \\
\text{\textdagger} & | \\
[-a\text{F}] & [a\text{F}]
\end{array}
\qquad
\begin{array}{cc}
\text{X} & \text{X} \\
 & | \\
 & [a\text{F}]
\end{array}
$$

1.6 Overview

In the chapters that follow, three major aspects of the phonology of Shilluk are discussed. Chapter 2 deals with the phonetic data and the phonological rules which apply postlexically, in which a brief phonemic analysis is presented. Chapter 3 is a brief grammatical account which establishes necessary morphosyntactic terminology followed by an examination of the underlying representation of words in the lexicon. There are obvious similarities between singular and plural words as well as between certain pairs of transitive verb forms. Despite similarities, however, vowel and tone differences turn out to be unpredictable. It is thus necessary to posit pairs of independent underlying representations for these forms which I shall term FORM 1 and FORM 2.

This argument is carried further in chapter 4. In the discussion of syllable structure, we see that even the number of syllable elements in the underlying representation of FORM 1 may be different from that of FORM 2. It is hypothesized that there are two distinct underlying syllable structures available for roots in the language. One of these structures accounts for INVARIABLY-LONG-VOWEL words while the other explains vowels which are long in open syllables, but short in closed syllables. This second syllable structure also accounts for INVARIABLY-SHORT-VOWEL words. The evidence for this hypothesis is examined in some detail.

Chapter 5 looks at tone and harmony systems. Having ascertained the various rules which apply to Shilluk phonology, it is then possible to order those rules within the lexicon. Three lexical strata are posited within the Shilluk lexicon.

In the concluding chapter, there is a listing of all the relevant rules from previous chapters as they would occur in a derivation. The implications of separate underlying representations are also discussed in relation to child language acquisition.

2

Phonetics, Phonemics, and Postlexical Phonology

We may now begin an examination of Shilluk phonology. A phonetic transcription of a portion of text is shown below, with both literal and free translations to provide context. This text does not contain the entire phonetic inventory, but it provides an impression of the language. A more complete inventory is given below.

(31)   [–   ⁻   _   –   –   _   – –   ⁻ – –   _]
       [tʃə̱ŋ³ akʸɛl ɲimʸa   ki   ɲiwa   akɛt̪ʰa bə̱m]
       day   one   sister^my with stepsister^our PST^go Bam
       One day, my sister and stepsister went to Bam

       [⁻ –   _   _ –   ⁻   ˎ   –   _ _]
       [alɔk kal   bʷʊ̱ɲɔ̱   bɛ ŋʸɛw kɛ   dʒami]
       PST^is Kal   Bwunyo   to buy   some things
       which is called Kal Bwunyo to buy some things

       [–   ˏ ⁻   – –   –   –   _ _   _ ⁻ ⁻   ]
       [ki yi ɟoː ařɔːt̪   gɛn yi̱ ɲʷɔli̱   pa-ani̱]
       and on road PST^attack them by daughters^of place-this
       On the way, they were attacked by the daughters of this place.

---

³The unfamiliar underscore diacritic for some vocoids is the symbol used to indicate expanded pharynx. See §2.1.

19

Phonetics, Phonemics, and Postlexical Phonology

[- -   - -]
[ka gɛ ɲǝkʰǫ]
and they fought
And they fought.

[-   -   - - -   -   - -   - _]
[kɛ baŋ mɛnani, ŋʸiɲ mɔ gɛn awaːɲ]
and after that, money of them PST^lose
And so, their money was lost.

[- -   - - _   - - - _ -   - -]
[ka gɛ dǫːga paⁱtʃ akɛtʰi wɔn ki mɛⁱya]
and they return village PST^go we with mother^my
And they returned to the village and we went with my mother.

[-   -   - - -   -   -   -]
[ka tʸɛ̰ŋ pa-ani pʸɛç yḭ wɔn]
and people place-this ask by us
And the people of this place were asked by us,

[- _ - - -   - - -   -   -]
[kipaŋɔ ařɔːt̰   ot̰ɔŋɔ ki yoː]
why   PST^attack children on road
Why were our children attacked on the road

[- -   - - - - _]
[o gɛ nṵːdḭ tɔːŋa paⁱç]
and they not^yet go^to village
since they had not yet reached the village?

[- _   - -   - -   _   -   -]
[ka dʑiː pa-ani řḭːŋa wǫk ki lwak]
and people place-this run^to outside from barn
And the people of this village ran out from the barn

[- _   -   ╲]
[ki ɟok ma gḭːř]
with men which many
with many men.

Shilluk Phonology   21

```
[ -    _    -    -    ⌏    -    -    _    -    ]
[dɛ  bʊ̰ŋ kʷɔp ma  dɔ̰iʃ ma  lwɔp yḭ  gɛn ]
but  no   talk which good which speak by  them
But there was no use talking to them.
```

```
[ -    _ _    _    _    -    ]
[gɛ  yɔ̰:dḭ bɛⁱ tʃaⁱ wɔn. ]
they begin to   blame us
They began to blame us.
```

2.1 Phonetic inventory

To begin the discussion of Shilluk phonetics, a phonetic inventory is presented in (32) and (33).

(32)   Vocoids

| | Front | Back | |
	Unrounded	Unrounded	Rounded
high	i i: ḭ ḭ:		ʊ̰ ʊ ʊ:
		ə̰	o o: o̰ o̰:
low	ɛ æ: ɛ̰ ɛ̰:	a a: a̰:	ɔ ɔ:

Phonetics, Phonemics, and Postlexical Phonology

(33) Contoids

plosives	p	ṭ	t	c	k
	pʰ	ṭʰ	tʰ		kʰ
	pʸ	ṭʸ	tʸ		kʸ
	pʷ	ṭʷ	tʷ		kʷ
	b	ḍ	d	ɟ	g
	bʸ	ḍʸ	dʸ		gʸ
	bʷ	ḍʷ	dʷ	ɟʷ	gʷ
nasals	m	ṇ	n	ɲ	ŋ
	ṃ[4]	ṇ̣	ṇ	ɲ̣	ŋ̣
	mʸ			ɲʸ	ŋʸ
	mʷ		nʷ	ɲʷ	ŋʷ
fricatives	f		ʃ	ɕ	
	v			ʑ	
affricates			tʃ	tɕ	
			tʃʰ	tɕʰ	
			tʃʸ	tɕʸ	
			tʃʷ	tɕʷ	
			dʒ	dʑ	
			dʒʸ	dʑʸ	
			dʒʷ	dʑʷ	
liquids	w		l	y[5]	
	ẉ		ḷ	ỵ	
			lʸ		
			lʷ	yʷ	
vibrants			ř	r̃[6]	
			řʸ		

This rather large phonetic inventory is reduced to the phonemes listed in (34)–(35) by invoking the principle of contrast in identical or analogous environments (Pike 1947).

---

[4]The ( ) indicates a fortis production of this phone.

[5]The [y] symbol represents the palatal glide, not the front rounded close vowel as per the IPA.

[6]The [ř] and [r̃] represent the flapped and trilled vibrants, respectively.

Shilluk Phonology   23

(34)   Consonant contrasts

	Word	Gloss	Alternative pronunciations
/b/	bák	garden	
/c/	cak	to start	[cak, tʃak, tɕak, ʃak, ɕak]
/d/	dāk	pot	
/ḍ/	ḍɔ́k	mouth	
/g/	gɔ̀k	bracelet	
/ɟ/	ɟak	to rule	[ɟak, dʒak, dʑak]
/k/	kak	to split	
/l/	lɛ̂k	pestle	
/m/	mak	to catch	
/ɲ/	ɲâŋ	crocodile	
/ŋ/	ŋān	person	
/n/	nâm	river	
/ṇ/	àṇâṭ	type of fish	
/n/	ànā̱p	branch of tree	[ànā̱p, ànā̱f]
/ṇ/	ṭîṇ	small	
/n/	ṭin	today	
/t/	tɔ̀ŋ	spear	
/ṭ/	ṭɔ́l	rope	
/p/	pṳk	soft-shelled turtle	[pṳk, fṳk]
/b/	bṳk	to dig	[bṳk, vṳk]
/ř/	řɛ̂k	necklace	
/w/	wât	bull	
/y/	yɛp	to open	

(35)   Vowel contrasts for expanded pharynx

	[−EX]		[+EX]	
	Word	Gloss	Word	Gloss
/i/	bi	to come	bî̱	termite
	kī:	Nile River	kī̱:	falcon
/e/	yɛp	to open	yɛ́p	tail
	yɛ:yɔ	hair	yɛ:jɔ	rat
/a/	lʷaᵏ	barn	lʷā̱k	pride
	gâ:gɔ̄	button	ga:gɔ	to mock
/ɔ/	ḍɔ̀ŋɔ̀	Juba person	ḍɔ̱̂ŋɔ̱̀	basket
	gɔ̄:l	Wild Dog	gɔ̱́:l	fireplace in barn
/o/	dòt	tumble bugs	dṳt	loin cloth
	bò:ř	heat rash	bṳ:ř	hole

24   Phonetics, Phonemics, and Postlexical Phonology

(36)   Vowel contrasts for length

Short Vowel		Long Vowel	
Word	Gloss	Word	Gloss
cik	short (PL)	cí:k	discipline
kîc	orphan	kḭ̀:c	orphans
kwéř	small lizard	kwḛ̄:ř	small hoe
bʸḛdɔ̰	wrestling match	bʸḛ̀:lɔ́	stalk of millet
cak	to start	cà:k	milk
bə̰ɲɔ̰	refusal	bā̰:ɲɔ́	grasshopper
ʈɔ́l	rope	ʈɔ̄:l	ropes
àkɔ̰c	shorts	àkɔ̰:c	pairs of shorts
bot	slip on	bò:ř	heat rash
pṵ̀k	turtle	pṵ̄:k	waterpot

Note that [c] ~ [tʃ] ~ [tɕ] ~ [ɕ] ~ [ʃ] are all in free variation as are [ɟ] ~ [dʒ] ~ [dʑ], [p] ~ [f], and [b] ~ [v]. For convenience, these are symbolized as /c/, /ɟ/, /p/, and /b/, respectively.

High glides. The [ʸ] and [ʷ] could be interpreted as either palatalized and labialized consonants or as the first element of rising diphthongs. Since there are no vowel sequences in the language which do not involve a high vowel, this suggests that high glides are consonants rather than vowels. We will see later in §2.4 that rising diphthongs do occur in the language, but their behavior is quite different from that of these high glides.

It is, of course, possible to regard palatalized and labialized contoids as either single phonemes or as sequences of phonemes. The data relevant to this question are presented in (37).

Shilluk Phonology

(37)

c+y	Gloss	c+w	Gloss
bʸél	millet	bʷɔ̀lɔ̀	corn cob
cʸâŋ	sun	cʷāk	type of fish
dʸèl	goat	dʷɔ̄r	kudu, antelope
ḍʸaŋ	cow	ḍʷət	to rise
gʸèk	Nile lechwe	gʷɔ̄k	work
jʸák	2nd milking	jʷɔ̄k	sickness
kʸēɲ	horse	kʷéy	grandfather
lʸēc	elephant	lʷák	barn
àmʸél	stubborn	mʷɔl	morning
———		ònʷà:ŋɔ̀	black ants
ɲʸa:yɔ	fish trapped by flooding	ɲʷɛlɔ	earthworm
ŋʸɛl	to trundle	ŋʷéc	Nile monitor
pʸɛ̣w	heart	pʷɔ̀:ḍɔ̀	field
óřʸál	mongoose	———	
ótʸêm	dragonfly	ótʷēl	type of fish
ṭʸɛw	also	ṭʷɔ̄l	snake
———		yʷɔ̀t	flying termites

There are a few gaps in (37) which should be accounted for. The sequence [nʸ] seems to have merged with [ɲ]. Neither [ɳʸ] nor [ɳʷ] has been recorded. This may be because initial [ɳ] is rare. There is no reason to assume that they could not occur, however, and their absence is here considered the result of insufficient data. The only other sequences which may not occur are [řʷ], [wʸ], [yʸ] and [wʷ].

To account for palatalized and labialized contoids, we must consider several points. First, there is virtually no cooccurrence restriction on consonants. Secondly, there are no unambiguous sequences of consonants. In all stem-initial consonant clusters, the second element can only be a high glide.

Examples of *y* or *w* with adjacent vowel are presented in (38).

(38)

cy+v	Gloss	cw+v	Gloss
		ácwīk	hip joint
byél	millet	gwém	cheating
cyạ́:dɔ̀	likeness	cwà:gɔ̀	support
		cwɔ̣:gɔ̀	pretense
		cwòr	blind person
		obwʊ̣ɲɔ̣	foreigner

26 Phonetics, Phonemics, and Postlexical Phonology

These are the only kind of vocalic sequences that occur in the language. There are no unambiguous sequences of two vowels or three vowels. Both front and back vowels may occur with [y, w].

To summarize, there are no unambiguous sequences of vowels or consonants. There seems to be no obvious front or back restriction on the occurrence of vowels with /y/, even though there is limited distribution. There is virtually no restriction of occurrence between consonants and semivowels.

While this analysis is not compelling, it seems more economical from a phonological point of view to consider the consonant + semivowel as representing a sequence of consonants rather than as representing a distinct series of phonemes. It is also important to note that this sequence of consonant + glide only occurs initially in the root. We will see throughout this study that the root is an extremely important part of Shilluk words, and that recognizing the root is vital throughout the phonology.

There are two sequences which cannot occur as the onset of a Shilluk root; namely, *[rw], *[wy]. Further, the glide [y] cannot be followed by [i] or [i̪].

The basic phoneme inventory as it now stands is in (39).

(39)

p	ṭ	t	c	k
pʰ	ṭʰ	tʰ	cʰ	kʰ
b	ḍ	d	j	g
m	ṇ	n	ɲ	ŋ
m̰	ṇ̰	ṇ̰	ɲ̰	ŋ̰
w		l	y	
w̰		ḷ̰	y̰	
		ř ř̰		

Remaining contoids. Phones still unaccounted for are fortis contoids, the trilled vibrant, and aspirated plosives. We will deal with these in two sections. First I will deal with fortis contoids, and secondly with the plosives.

Fortis marking is here indicated by ( ) under the associated symbol. When these fortis consonants are said in slow, deliberate speech, they are, in fact, geminate or lengthened consonants. One Shilluk described the effect as similar to having a bit of glue on his tongue that held it to the roof of his mouth. In slow speech, these sounds are much like geminate consonants in Arabic. Once produced at normal speed, however, the

Shilluk Phonology   27

difference is certainly not one of length. Examples of slow speech and at normal speed are presented in (40).

(40)   slow speech   regular speed
       ṭal:a   ṭaḷa   'to cook'
       cíŋ:é   cíŋé   'his hands'

We could thus say that fortis consonants have two phonetic productions, one for slow, deliberate speech and one for normal or rapid speech. We might write the rule for this as in (41). Geminates may only be heard intervocalically; at the end of words, there are no geminate sonorants or nasals.

(41)   long sonorants → [m̥ n̥ n ɲ ŋ l r̃ w̥ y̥] / rapid speech
                          [m: n̥: n: ɲ: ŋ: l: r̃: w: y:] / deliberate speech

The only set of contoids left to consider are the plosives. We would expect that all plosives could be geminated. So, what is the phonetic realization of gemination in this case?

If we look at the root-final consonant of a plural word, we will find either a fortis sonorant or an aspirated plosive. When said in deliberate speech, the aspirated plosive is manifestly a geminate or lengthened plosive. Thus, we may conclude that intervocalically, double plosives are of long duration in slow speech and aspirated in normal speech.[7]

(42)   long plosives → [p: ṭ: t: c: k:] / intervocalic deliberate speech
                         [pʰ ṭʰ tʰ cʰ kʰ] / intervocalic normal speech

Since the [c] may also be produced as an affricate, [tʃ], it should be clarified that the lengthening is evidenced on the closure phase.

Usually in word-final position, plosives are voiceless. There is a regular rule of word-final devoicing such that all plosives become voiceless word-finally. The realization rule can be stated as follows.

---

[7]Different speakers have unconsciously demonstrated the phonetic qualities of double or geminate plosives. One speaker insisted the correct pronunciation of 'his hooves' was [dàt.té] while another said [dà.tʰé]. The dot (.) indicates a syllable break. The [t.t] was pronounced as [t:]. When a double consonant was written, all parties expressed enthusiastic approval.

28   Phonetics, Phonemics, and Postlexical Phonology

(43)   voiced plosives →   [p ṭ t c k] / word-finally

                        [b ḍ d j g] / elsewhere

(44)   voiceless plosives → [p ṭ t c k]

It has been decided that the palatalized and labialized consonants are sequences of phones, and so do not need to be included in our chart.

All phones of the phonetic inventory have now been accounted for. The resulting Shilluk consonants are listed in (45), at five phonetically relevant points of articulation—bilabial, dental, alveolar, palatal, and velar. There are oral (voiced and voiceless) and nasal plosives and a set of non-nasal sonorants.

(45)   plosives   voiceless   p   ṭ   t   c   k

                  voiced   b   ḍ   d   j   g

      nasals   m   ṇ   n   ɲ   ŋ

      liquids   (w)   l   y   (w)

      vibrant   r

Vocoids. There are ten vowels in the Shilluk vowel system. They may be divided into two sets according to the feature of expanded pharynx [±EX].

The term advanced tongue root [ATR] has been employed in some languages to describe this phenomenon. However, the term Expanded Pharynx (Lindau 1979) seems to be more accurate for Shilluk. The [+EX] vowels are distinguished acoustically or impressionistically by a muffled or breathy quality while the [−EX] vowels have been described as brassy (Jacobson 1980). Most of the front vowels are phonetically similar in vowel height; the back vowels differ somewhat.

(46)   [−EX]   [+EX]

      i   o   i̱   u̱

      ɛ   ɔ   ɛ̱   o̱

          a   ə̱

In this study, the [+EX] value will be indicated by an underscore on all vowels, and the vowel symbols will be [i e a ɔ o u]. [ɛ] and [ɛ̱] will be written as /e/ and /e̱/; /o̱/ is written as /ɔ̱/. (47) uses the symbols as they will appear in this study.

Shilluk Phonology   29

(47)   [−EX]   [+EX]
        i   o   i̠   u̠
        e   ɔ   e̠   ɔ̠
             a   a̠

Each of these ten vowels may also be lengthened. We have seen that each one contrasts in identical or near identical environments from (36). (48) is a phonemic inventory of vowel phonemes.

(48)   Vowel phonemes

	Front		Back	
	Unrounded		Unrounded	Rounded
High	i i: i̠ i̠:			o o: u̠ u̠:
Low	e e: e̠ e̠:		a a: a̠ a̠:	ɔ ɔ: ɔ̠ ɔ̠:

We may account for the remaining phones by the following rules.

(49)   Vowel phonemes
        /e:/→ [æ:]
        /a̠/ → [ə]
        /ɔ̠/ → [o̠]
        /u/ → [ʋ] / ___ nasal consonant

Having identified the phonemes of Shilluk, there are still some un-answered questions. Taxonomic phonemics asks What?, not Why? In order to capture the generalizations in Shilluk, we turn to generative phonology and begin by establishing the distinctive features of Shilluk.

2.2 Classificatory features

The matrix in (50) shows the consonantal features listed along with the ± values. After the matrix, the justification for each of the features is given. Finally, the minimal feature matrix is given along with the relevant rules.

(50)

	VOC	VOI	SON	NAS	CCL	OCC	VIB	RND	LAB	API	COR	HI
p	−	−	−	−	+	+	−	−	+	−	−	−
b	−	+	−	−	+	+	−	−	+	−	−	−
ṭ	−	−	−	−	+	+	−	−	−	+	+	−
ḍ	−	+	−	−	+	+	−	−	−	+	+	−
t	−	−	−	−	+	+	−	−	−	−	+	−
d	−	+	−	−	+	+	−	−	−	−	+	−
c	−	−	−	−	+	+	−	−	−	−	+	+
j	−	+	−	−	+	+	−	−	−	−	+	+
k	−	−	−	−	+	+	−	−	−	−	−	+
g	−	+	−	−	+	+	−	−	−	−	−	+
m	−	+	+	+	+	+	−	−	+	−	−	−
ṇ	−	+	+	+	+	+	−	−	−	+	+	−
n	−	+	+	+	+	+	−	−	−	−	+	−
ɲ	−	+	+	+	+	+	−	−	−	−	+	+
ŋ	−	+	+	+	+	+	−	−	−	−	−	+
w	+	+	+	−	−	−	−	+	+	−	−	+
y	+	+	+	−	−	−	−	−	−	−	+	+
l	−	+	+	−	+	−	−	−	−	−	+	−
r	−	+	+	−	+	−	+	−	−	−	+	−

The features have been used because of the morphological processes involved. Sommerstein (1977:97) has said that "The criterion of morphophonemic relevance is...of more value in confirming the systematic status of a feature than in disconfirming it."

The first feature listed in the matrix is [VOC] or vocalic. If the analysis were linear, the feature [consonantal] would need to be included, but within the nonlinear framework, the syllable structure defines the consonants and vowels. When [w] or [y] occur, the [+VOC] feature is sufficient identification, and the syllable structure defines it as a consonant. The feature [VOC] is retained in order to discuss the glides which occur in stem onsets.

The voicing feature, [VOI] is needed to distinguish the voiced and voiceless plosives. The sonorant [SON] feature separates plosives in Shilluk from all the other phonemes. There is good evidence that plosives in the language behave in a very different way from other consonants. It is necessary to distinguish nasal [NAS] as a separate class within the [SON] class because there is an interesting interaction between [NAS] and non-nasal stops which needs to be captured.

There is strong morphophonemic evidence that the features central closure [CCL] and occlusive [OCC] are needed. [CCL] is defined by Sommerstein as a complete closure involving the center of the oral tract. By

Shilluk Phonology

contrast, [OCC] blocks the flow of air in the mouth. Thus, the feature [OCC] provides a useful category for discussing the alternation between plosives and nasals seen in §5.3, examples (401)–(402). The [OCC] feature excludes the [l r] which do not participate in the process.

There is another alternation between /l r/ and /d/ discussed in §3.2. Without the feature [CCL] there would be no natural class defined for this morphological interaction. /l/ and /r/ are distinguished from each other by the feature vibrant [VIB].

/w/ and /y/ are distinguished by the features [LAB] (for /w/) and [COR] (for /y/). The feature [RND] is not necessary for the consonants, though it is used in the vowel feature matrix. In order for /w/ and /u/ to have the same feature specification, the feature [RND] has been included in the consonant feature matrix.

Now we come to the point of articulation features. The features labial [LAB], apical [API], coronal [COR], and high [HI] have been set up. The feature anterior has not been used because there are no processes which necessarily link [LAB] with [API] and/or [COR]. There is a phonotactic constraint that affects all [+COR, +OCC] segments; namely, one that concerns the feature [±API]. The tip of the tongue is decidedly the important factor separating the dental and alveolar [+OCC] segments. For these reasons, [COR] seems to be a more relevant category than [ANTERIOR]. The combination of [COR] and [HI] will distinguish the palatals. The velars are [−COR] and [+HI].

The features specified for vowels ideally should be the same as for consonants and vice versa according to the FEATURE MINIMALIZATION PRINCIPLE (Archangeli, 1984:50). According to this principle, it is most desirable to include the minimal number of features necessary to differentiate between the phonemes of the language.

The features used for the vowel system are [HI], low [LO] and [RND]. [HI] is used with the consonants. Though there are no [LO] consonants in Shilluk, the use of [LO] seems unavoidable in the vowels. Round is being used redundantly for the consonants because it is needed for the vowels. Back could have been chosen for the vowels, but this feature would have been less relevant to the consonants. Thus, the /u/ and /i/ have the same specifications as the /w/ and /y/; namely, [+HI, +RND] and [+HI, −RND] respectively. [EX] distinguishs the two sets of vowels though it is not shown in the matrix because all vowels are either [±EX]. The assignment of the [EX] feature is made in the lexicon. Let us now consider the feature matrix for vowels.

(51)

	HI	LO	RND
i	+	−	−
e	−	−	−
a	−	+	−
ɔ	−	−	+
o	+	−	+

2.3 Redundancy rules

Much of the information contained in such a fully specifed matrix is often nondistinctive or redundant. It is desirable to select the most fundamental differences between the representations for the underlying representation. The redundancies can then be supplied by redundancy rules which are in part universal. The universal rules are COST FREE since they do not need to be LEARNED.

The theory of underspecification developed by Archangeli (1984) argues for including only the bare minimum of information. A fuller account of UNDERSPECIFICATION THEORY is found in §1.2. The features to be specified are given in the DISTINCTIVE FEATURE MATRIX. The unspecified features are filled in by either a COMPLEMENT RULE or a DEFAULT RULE.

One of the advantages of underspecification theory is the way in which it explains the asymmetric behavior of certain consonants or vowels. For example, an epenthetic vowel is considered to be the maximally underspecified vowel. At the end of the derivation, it receives its specification and appears by default on all empty syllable heads. We will find this concept helpful as we look at Shilluk. First, though, let us examine an underspecified matrix for Shilluk consonants.

Shilluk Phonology

(52)

	VOC	VOI	SON	NAS	CCL	OCC	VIB	RND	LAB	API	COR	HI
p						+			+			
b		+				+			+			
ṯ						+				+		
ḍ		+				+				+		
t						+					+	−
d		+				+					+	−
c						+					+	
j		+				+					+	
k						+						
g		+				+						
m				+					+			
ṇ				+						+		
n				+							+	−
ɲ				+							+	
ŋ				+								
w	+								+			
y	+										+	
l			+		+						+	
r							+					

The minimally specified consonant in Shilluk is /k/. My justification for this analysis is based on the observation that /k/ often does not appear on the surface where it is expected. For example, in the phrase *arum ki +* (verb), production in normal speech is *arᴜmi_____* 'someone finished _____ing'.

In another common phrase *ḍɔ cɔl:ɔ* 'Shilluk language' the literal meaning is 'mouth of the Shilluk'. Since the word for mouth is *ḍok*, it suggests that underlyingly *ḍɔ cɔl:ɔ* is /ḍɔk cɔl:ɔ/. A similar elision occurs with the word for 'door' or 'mouth of the house' where /ḍɔk ɔt/ surfaces as *ḍɔ ɔt*. When asked to produce the phrases mentioned in a word-for-word fashion, /k/ reappears. There seems to be no objection to writing the /k/ even though it is not normally pronounced. People seem to acknowledge its underlying presence.

Given the assumption that /k/ is the underspecified consonant, we have the following redundancy rules for Shilluk. The COMPLEMENT RULES (CR) and DEFAULT RULES (DR) are labelled.

(53)

[ ] → [−VIB]		CR
[ ] → [−HI] / [+$\overline{\text{VIB}}$]		DR
[ ] → [−OCC] / [+$\overline{\text{VIB}}$]		DR
[ ] → [+CCL] / [+$\overline{\text{VIB}}$]		DR
[ ] → [+SON] / [+$\overline{\text{VIB}}$]		DR
[ ] → [+COR] / [+$\overline{\text{VIB}}$]		DR
[ ] → [−VOC]		CR
[ ] → [−CCL] / [+$\overline{\text{VOC}}$]		DR
[ ] → [+SON] / [+$\overline{\text{VOC}}$]		DR
[ ] → [−OCC] / [+$\overline{\text{VOC}}$]		DR
[ ] → [−LAB]		CR
[ ] → [+RND] / $\begin{bmatrix} +\overline{\text{VOC}} \\ +\text{LAB} \end{bmatrix}$		DR
[ ] → [−HI] / $\begin{bmatrix} -\overline{\text{VOC}} \\ +\text{LAB} \end{bmatrix}$		DR
[ ] → [−API]		CR
[ ] → [−HI] / [+$\overline{\text{API}}$]		DR
[ ] → [+COR] / [+$\overline{\text{API}}$]		DR

[ ] → [−NAS]		CR
[ ] → [+SON] / [+$\overline{\text{NAS}}$]		DR
[ ] → [−SON]		CR
[ ] → [+VOI] / [+$\overline{\text{SON}}$]		DR
[ ] → [−OCC]		CR
[ ] → [+OCC] / [+$\overline{\text{NAS}}$]		DR
[ ] → [+CCL] / [+$\overline{\text{OCC}}$]		DR
[ ] → [−HI] / $\begin{bmatrix} +\overline{\text{SON}} \\ +\text{CCL} \\ -\text{NAS} \end{bmatrix}$		DR
[ ] → [−VOI]		CR
[ ] → [−RND]		CR
[ ] → [−COR]		CR
[ ] → [+HI]		CR

The UNDERSPECIFIED MATRIX for the vowels is much simpler. The maximally underspecified vowel is /i/. There are two main reasons for proposing this analysis. First, /i/ tends to be the least stable vowel. In the monosyllabification process that seems to be at work in the language, the /i/ is the vowel most easily lost. The PLURAL I INCORPORATION process, described in detail in chapter 4, involves moving an -i plural suffix into the root of the word. However, the -i never surfaces as [i] after this process. The syllable structure of the word changes, thus giving evidence of its presence, but it takes on the features of the root vowel. As a maximally underspecified vowel, it can be seen as having no features of its own. Therefore, it is reasonable to assume that it would simply acquire features by assimilating the features of the vowel with which it shares a syllable head.

The second reason for positing /i/ as the maximally underspecified vowel is its epenthetic behavior. While epenthesis is not a regular process of the language, in rapid speech an /i/ is often inserted to separate consonants. When the same sequence is repeated in slow speech, the /i/ is no longer present, but a slight pause will separate the consonants.

Shilluk Phonology

Another point that should be made is that the same CR is needed for both the /k/ and the /i/; namely, [ ] → [+HI]. This CR is independently motivated for both segments.

Finally, the articulatory setting for Shilluk provides one further argument in favor of nonspecified status for the /i/. The Shilluk people often remove their lower incisors at puberty. As a result of this physical alteration, the tongue tip shifts forward thus placing the body of the tongue in a more palatal position. This articulatory setting seems to parallel the [+HI] feature for both the nonspecified segment for the vowel and the minimally specified segment for the consonant.

The underspecified feature matrix for Shilluk vowels is given below. Again, the [EX] feature is not included in the matrix since it is lexically assigned and may apply equally to all vowels.

(54)

	HI	LO	RND
i			
e	−		−
a		+	
ɔ	−		+
o	+		

The redundancy rules for vowels are:

(55)

$$[\ ] \rightarrow [-\text{LO}] \qquad\qquad\qquad\quad \text{CR}$$
$$[\ ] \rightarrow [-\text{HI}] \ / \ [+\overline{\text{LO}}] \quad \text{DR}$$
$$[\ ] \rightarrow [-\text{RND}] \qquad\qquad\qquad \text{CR}$$
$$[\ ] \rightarrow [+\text{HI}] \qquad\qquad\qquad\quad \text{CR}$$

2.4 Nonlinear analysis

The problem with a segmental analysis is that the phonological representation has been oversimplified (van der Hulst and Smith, 1982:3). A nonlinear analysis allows us the freedom to develop these representations to a greater extent. The end result provides more explanatory power as we capture the generalizations that would otherwise be missed.

Constraints for the onset of the root can now be stated in nonlinear terms. We begin with the INITIAL CONSONANT SEQUENCE[8] which allows for glides to follow consonants at the beginning of a root morpheme.

(56)   INITIAL CONSONANT SEQUENCE (ICS)

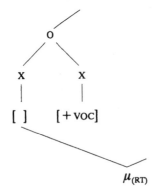

Two constraints are placed on the initial root sequences.

(57)   INITIAL CONSONANT SEQUENCE CONSTRAINT (ICSC)

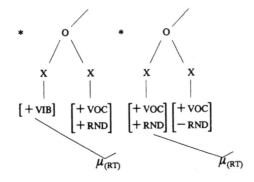

These two constraints disallow the sequences *[rw] and *[wy]. There is a further constraint with regard to the glide and the following vowel. This constraint is shown in (58), where the [y] glide may only be followed by a vowel which is [−HI, −RND].

---

[8]For the reader's convenience, an alphabetized listing of abbreviations, example number and name of rule or constraint discussed within each chapter is shown at the end of that chapter.

Shilluk Phonology

(58) GLIDE AND VOWEL CONSTRAINT (GVC)

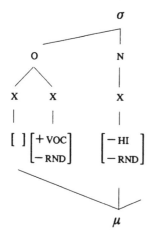

One new feature, [TENSE], is introduced. It is important to point out that this feature does not belong in the CLASSIFICATORY MATRIX. This particular feature is relevant only at the postlexical level. According to the principle of structure preservation, new phonemes are not allowed to appear at the lexical level. However, post-lexically, new phonetic sounds are permitted. Since this feature cannot be generally applied throughout the phonology as can the other features, we recognize it as a late-comer which can come into operation only at either the postlexical or phonetic levels.

Geminates. We begin our analysis by looking at gemination of consonants. We want to investigate particularly the factors that relate to the fortis realization of geminate consonants.

Hock (1986) states that in the cases of Hindi and Western Germanic, geminate consonants are more FORTIS than single segments. In Shilluk the relationship between a geminate consonant and the feature [TENSE] needs to be considered. First, we have a TENSING RULE which introduces the feature [+TNS] with geminate consonants.

(59) TENSING RULE (TR)

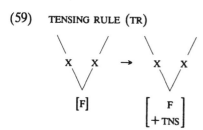

This rule applies to *any* geminate consonants in addition to the vibrants, so long as we understand that the [r̃] is [+TNS] while the [r̆] is [−TNS]. However, to deal with the other sonorants and nasals, we need a further rule which accounts for the phonetic shortening of these [+TNS] consonants. Consider the rule in (60).

(60) PHONETIC SHORTENING RULE (PSR)

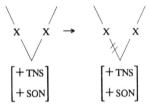

The TENSING RULE is intrinsically ordered before the SHORTENING RULE in a feeding relationship. Sonorants (including nasals) which are [+TNS] are shortened in normal speech. They maintain their [+TNS] feature which is realized by a fortis production. Let us look at some sample derivations using these rules.

(61)   /ciŋŋ + e/ 'his hands'   /ader̃r̃e/ 'his donkeys'
     TR   ciɲɲe   ader̃r̃e
     PSR   ciɲe   ———
     SF   [ciɲe]   [ader̃e]

Gemination is not uncommon in Nilotic languages. Recent studies have shown that gemination appears in Anywak (Reh, personal communication), Alur (Kutsch Lojenga, personal communication), Lotuho (Coates, 1985), and Mabaan (Walker, personal communication). There is also further evidence from plosives in Dinka that would indicate the presence of underlying geminates (Duerkson, personal communication).

These geminates are not usually characterized by increased duration. Consonants are described in Lotuho as being STRONG or WEAK, but certainly *not* long or short.[9] (Hollman, personal communication and Coates, 1985). In Alur, the geminate plosives are realized as voiceless aspirated consonants with no special feature of increased length. Thus, we are not suggesting something new, but simply proposing an analysis that has not been previously argued for in Shilluk.

---

[9]In her paper, Coates used [y:] and [w:] to indicate STRONG consonants. In personal communication, she confirmed that strong consonants are fortis productions and that the colon does not indicate length.

Shilluk Phonology

Shilluk has distinctive length within the vowel system. It is not implausible, then, that this feature of length would also be evident in the consonant system.

While geminate consonants have a unique phonetic realization in Shilluk, it is not being suggested at this point, that this realization is relevant to the classificatory matrix. In fact, the contrast is a structural one in which a set of features is assigned to either one or two x slots.

It is still possible to hear both fortis consonants and lengthened consonants from the same speaker in the same words—spoken at different rates. In years to come, that distinction may be lost at which point, the fortis productions may become part of the phonological system. For the present, however, we are still able to see the relationship between the segmental feature [TNS] and the multitiered representation of gemination.

(62)   x   x
         \   /
          \   /
           \ /
         [+TNS]

This association of [TNS] and gemination is somewhat parallel to the case of differential vowel length before voiced and voiceless stops in English. The plosive voicing is what is thought to be the distinguishing feature. However, the real clue lies in the vowel length.

     rope   robe
     [o]   [oː]

With Shilluk, the feature [TNS] may become distinctive in the future, but for now it is only needed in a phonetic feature matrix.

Plosives. We turn our attention now to the plosives. First, there is a postlexical rule which devoices all plosives syllable-finally. In actual fact, this process can be described at a syllable level where plosives in coda position are devoiced.

(63)   SYLLABLE-FINAL DEVOICING (SFD)

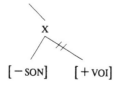

40 Phonetics, Phonemics, and Postlexical Phonology

There are underlyingly voiceless plosives which would surface as voiceless even in syllable onset position. Underlyingly voiced plosives would surface as voiced in syllable onset position. Example (64) shows some voiceless plosives and (65) gives an example of the SFD rule.

(64)   *búkɔ̰*   'Khartoum'
          ànwàtɔ   'white worm'

(65)   /leb/   →   lep   →   [lep]   'tongue'
              SFD   SF

Hock (1986) says that the fortis characteristic is also responsible for devoicing such that [+TNS] tends to imply [−VOI]. This tendency is certainly evident in Shilluk plosives. The following rule for Shilluk shows that [−SON, +TNS] consonants are associated with [−VOI].

(66)   TENSE-VOICING RULE (TVR)

$$[+\text{VOI}]$$
$$\overset{|}{\not{|}}$$
$$\text{x}$$
$$|$$
$$\begin{bmatrix} +\text{TNS} \\ -\text{SON} \end{bmatrix}$$

This rule says that if a [−SON] consonant is associated with the feature [+TNS], and also associated with [+VOI], the voicing is delinked. The result of this delinking is a voiceless plosive. For ease of notation, the rule is stated with a single rather than a double x.

In order to prevent geminate consonants from occurring in the root-initial position, one further constraint needs to be formulated whereby geminate consonants cannot occur in the onset position within a root morpheme.

Shilluk Phonology 41

(67) INITIAL GEMINATE CONSONANT SEQUENCE CONSTRAINT (IGCSC)

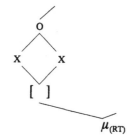

Intervocalic plosives are not only voiceless, but also aspirated. Presumably this INTERVOCALIC ASPIRATION RULE applies after the TENSING RULE in (66). The aspiration can be looked upon as a delinking of the [−SON] feature. The [−VOI] is retained while the vowel features spread to the left from the nucleus creating the aspiration. The rule is given below.

(68) INTERVOCALIC ASPIRATION RULE (IAR)

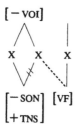

Below, these rules are working together to derive the surface plosive consonants.

(69) /dadd + e/ 'its hooves'   /daadd/ 'hooves'
  TR   daṭṭe   daaṭṭ
  CSP ———   daaṭ (see (237))
  IAR daṭʰe   ———
  SF   [daṭʰe]   [daːṭ]

(70) /dud̪/ 'loin cloth'   /dud̪ + e/ 'his loin cloth'
  SFD dut̪   ———
  SF   [dut̪]   [dud̪e]

In summary, all geminate consonants undergo the TENSING RULE (59). The [+SON] geminates also undergo the PHONETIC SHORTENING RULE (60). The result is a short, fortis consonant.

The plosives, [−SON], on the other hand, undergo the TENSE-VOICING RULE (66) after the TENSING RULE (59). The devoiced plosive is then aspirated intervocalically by the INTERVOCALIC ASPIRATION RULE (68). For syllable-final geminate plosives, it is unclear at this time whether the TVR applies before or after the syllabification principle found in chapter 4 (CSP, (237)). There is some evidence to suggest that degeminated final plosives are unreleased while single plosives have a light release. If the CSP applies first, before the TENSING RULE, then the release should be the same for single and geminate root-final plosives. However, if there is a released/unreleased contrast, it would mean that the TENSING RULE applies before the CSP which delinks one of the timing slots for the geminate consonants in a coda slot of the syllable. Further investigation into this area is needed.

Phonetic rules for vowels. Two phonetic rules need to be stated for Shilluk vowels. The first of these is a rule to insert an on-glide.

(71)   DIPHTHONG HIGH SPREADING RULE (DHSR)

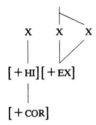

In this rule, the [HI] feature spreads from the root-initial palatal consonant onto the nucleus which has the feature [+EX]. It is also a requirement that the nucleus be realized as a long vowel. This inserted glide is a phonetic transition from the palatal consonant into the vowel, i.e., a rising diphthong. This diphthong should not be confused with the semi-vowel in the complex onset. At the phonetic level, the difference is neutralized. However, in environments where the vowel shortens, the underlying difference is apparent. The [y] will remain with a shortened [+EX] vowel whereas the [i] on-glide, or rising diphthong, will disappear because the conditions for its appearance are no longer present.

Shilluk Phonology

(72) OFF-GLIDE HIGH SPREADING RULE (OHSR)

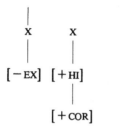

The second rule is the OFF-GLIDE HIGH SPREADING RULE. Its conditions are almost the reverse of the ones for the on-glide. This rule allows for [HI] spreading from the palatal consonant to the [−EX] vowel to its left. The nucleus must be realized as a short vowel for this rule to apply. Again, the transient nature of this rule is seen when the vowel is lengthened: the off-glide is no longer present when the [−EX] vowel is long. Below are examples of both the rising diphthong and the off-glide.

(73) UF   Rule   SF
     /yeejɔ/   DHSR   [yⁱeːjɔ]   'rat'
     /ɲaalɔ/   DHSR   [ɲⁱaːlɔ]   'reticulate python'
     /mac/   OHSR   [maⁱc]   'fire'
     /lɔɲ/   OHSR   [lɔⁱɲ]   'small animal'

Vowel length. Shilluk has four phonetic degrees of length. The [+EX] vowels tend to be longer than the [−EX] set. Phonemically, there are two degrees of vowel length.

(74) gɔ́l   'household'
      gɔ́ːl   'wild dog'
      áŋūn   'sickle'
      áŋūːŋ   'mucous'

The explanation of phonemic vowel length is somewhat complicated. There are underlying short vowels and long vowels as well as a third set which is underlyingly long, but which is sensitive to a shortening rule within a closed syllable. This phenomenon is dealt with in chapter 4. Length is not considered to be a distinctive feature in Shilluk. Instead, length differences are handled by means of a structural distinction using x slots. There is no phonetic difference in the length of vowels that shorten in closed syllables and those that do not shorten.

44 Phonetics, Phonemics, and Postlexical Phonology

(75)
	Front	Back	
	Unrounded	Unrounded	Rounded
High	i i̠		o u̠
	e e̠		ɔ ɔ̠
Low		a a̠	

The underscored vowels are [+EX] while the /i e a ɔ o/ are [−EX]. All vowels may be long or short.

2.5. Phonetic tone

On the surface, Shilluk has three distinctive pitch levels. These three may be termed high, mid, and low (H M L). The interval between H and M seems to be approximately equal to the interval between M and L. Thus, between H and L, we find two intervals. These relative intervals may be shown in a diagrammatic pitch notation as shown in (76).

(76) HM [⁻ –] ML [– _] HL [⁻ _]
    MH [– ⁻] LM [_ –] LH [_ ⁻]

For a given speaker, the absolute level of each distinctive pitch is maintained fairly consistently throughout an utterance as shown below.

(77) [– ⁻ _⁻⁻ – – ⁻]
    ka tyeŋ pa-ani pyɛc yi̠ wɔn
    And the people of this village were asked by us.

(78) [⁻ _ _ _ _ _ ⁻]
    ge yɔ̠:ti be cayi wɔn
    They began to blame us.

All of the H's in (77) are realized on much the same pitch, as are all the M's. In (78) the L's are all on the same pitch as well with the H at the end realized higher than the initial M. It is concluded, therefore, that there is no downdrift nor any automatic downstep.

An attempt will be made to account for the three pitches in terms of two underlying tones. However, we will see in the end that the three pitch levels in Shilluk correspond underlyingly to three level tones. Let us begin our discussion by an examination of the data.

Shilluk Phonology   45

There are contrasts among all three pitch levels in one-syllable words.
Example (79) has [−EX] vowels, (80) has the C + semivowel onset, and
(81) has [+EX] vowels.

(79) H   bák   'garden'
      M   bāɲ   'cow with drooping horns'
      L   bàk   'guess!'

(80) H   byél   'millet (PL)'
      M   byēr   'roots'
      L   byèl   'carry!'

(81) H   ḳə́r   'wealthy'
      M   ḳāc   'hunger'
      L   ḳə̀p   'raid'

There are two types of two-syllable words in Shilluk. Beginning with the
prefix + root and then moving on to words with the pattern of root +
suffix, we will look at their differences. (The term root in this thesis has a
specialized meaning which is discussed in §5.1.)

In the examples below, we find the following sequences of tones H-H,
H-M, H-L, M-L, L-H, L-M, L-L.

(82) HH   álám   'dragnet'
      HM   átwēl   'stem of plant'
      HL   ágàk   'raven'
      ML   ādwɔ̀k   'gum trees'
      LH   àḍúṭ   'stinger of bee'
      LM   àbɔ̄y   'rotten fish'
      LL   àdwɔ̀l   'grain'

The a- prefix may be H, M, or L. The root may also be H, M, or L so long
as the prefix is H or L. If the prefix is M, the only possible root tone is L.
This is an interesting restriction which we will need to keep in mind in the
following discussion of M tone.

In order to see the patterns more clearly, a matrix is presented in (83). The
tones indicated on the left are prefix tones. Across the top are the root tones.
An X means that the combination of prefix and root tones is possible.

46   Phonetics, Phonemics, and Postlexical Phonology

(83)   Root tones

		H	M	L
Prefix	H	X	X	X
tones	M			X
	L	X	X	X

Before discussing these patterns, we need to complete the data with root + suffix tone patterns.

(84)

HH	dɔ́:rɔ́	'axe'
HM	gám:į̄	'midwives'
HL	búḍɔ̀	'zucchini'
MM	dō:dɔ̄	'tumble bug'
LL	dwà:lɔ̀	'fat'
LH	byè:lɔ́	'stalk of millet'

In these words, we see a rather more limited distribution. The root tone may be H, M, or L but the occurrence of suffix tones with these root tones seems rather restricted. The matrix (85) reveals what is missing.

(85)   Root tone

H	M	L		
X		X	H	Suffix
X	X		M	tone
X		X	L	

Most of the restrictions involve the M tone. M root tone cannot take H or L suffix tone. Also, L root tone cannot be followed by M on the suffix.

Let us examine three-syllable words in the data below. The only level tones which occur are listed here.

(86)

HLL	ácừŋɔ̀	'black mound termite'
LMH	àbā:rɔ́	'fencing grass'
LLL	àdừdɔ̀	'large sieve'

Distribution of tones is severely limited in these three-syllable words. Compound words are not within the scope of this study so their tone patterns will not enter into this discussion.

It is interesting that the number of tone combinations decreases as the number of syllables increases. This is contrary to what would be expected. With three tones on two-syllable words, we could expect nine possible tone combinations. With the same three tones on three-syllable words, there

Shilluk Phonology   47

could be as many as twenty-seven potential patterns. In Shilluk, there are
only three patterns with level tones in three-syllable words.

Perhaps the phenomenon can be explained by positing two tones in the
underlying representation. If we can adequately account for surface [H M L]
by this means, then it might explain the relatively few tone patterns in
three-syllable words.

2.6. Interpretation of tone

In the literature, it is pointed out that there are various ways to account
for three surface pitch levels in terms of two tones. We will look at four
of these: assimilation, dissimilation, upstep, and downstep. Each of these
approaches will be considered in turn.

Assimilation. Schuh (1978:230) says of assimilation that tones "remain
in their original segmental domain but become more like (perhaps identical
to) neighboring tones". It is possible to account for a M tone by assimilating L→M/__H or H→M/__L.

If that is the case, then there should be no distinction between L and M
before H or between H and M before L. We see that is not the case from
(87).

(87)	+*ání*		Tone
dɔ́:rɔ́	*dɔ́:rá ní*	'axe'	[¯ ¯ ¯]
gɔ̄:lɔ̄	*gɔ̄:láni*	'hook'	[– – ¯]
lè:lɔ̀	*lè:láni*	'stone'	[_ ¯ ¯]

H, M, and L all contrast in the environment of H. According to the
principle of assimilation, if /gɔɔlɔ/ was actually associated with L tone, then
it would be raised to M because of the following H tone. However, we see
in the word /leelɔ/ that it begins L and continues L even in the environment
of H. But let us look a bit further.

The possessive marker on a semantically singular noun consistently has
M tone. By contrast, semantically plural nouns have a possessive marker
with H tone. As we have already seen that all three tones contrast with H
in (87) only data relating to the singular followed by M tone will be given.

48   Phonetics, Phonemics, and Postlexical Phonology

(88)   + 3s PS   Tone
    dɔ́:rɔ́   dɔ́:rē   'axe '   [− −]
    gɔ́:lɔ́   gɔ́:lē   'hook'   [− −]
    lè:lɔ́   lè:lē   'stone'   [_ −]

H, M, and L tones all occur with the M suffix tone. As assimilation is
unable to account for M tone, we reject any theory involving assimilation
and turn to dissimilation and polarization.

Dissimilation and polarization. In Schuh's discussion, dissimilation assumes there is an underlying tone which changes by a rule such as [+H]
→ [−H]/[+H]__. Polarization, on the other hand, applies to syllables with
no underlying tone. A rule is posited to supply the unspecified tone such
as tone → [−αH]/[αH] __. Schuh states that in both cases, these rules are
morphological and words must be marked if they are to undergo the rules.
They do not apply as general phonological rules.
    Given the frequency of M tone in Shilluk and the fact that any sequence
of tones may occur, it would be uneconomical to have to specify every
occurrence of a rule application to account for it. It is unlikely that
dissimilation or polarity accounts for the third tone.

Upstep. Upstep is a rare phenomenon in the world's languages. Anderson (1978) cites two examples from the literature. An upstep language
raises tones in a sequence of progressively higher tones. If we posit that a
H tone raises any subsequent tone, then we could say that a [HM] tone is
/HL/ underlyingly. Our argument would fail because [HM] contrasts with [HL]
in Shilluk.
    Upstep should raise a following L, at least higher than a preceding L.
However, we see in (89) that the L's are the same level.

(89)   [_ ˉ _]   àbàṭúrɔ̀   'Nile monitor lizard'
        [ˉ _ _]   áwàrtáwà: 'day before yesterday'

Thus, we cannot invoke upstep to account for M tone.

Downstep. The literature is filled with accounts of languages with three
or four pitches being analyzed as processes involving downstep (DS)
(Anderson 1978, Hyman 1979 and 1985b, Goldsmith 1976, Clements and
Ford 1981). There are so many possibilities that it is difficult to tell
whether a language has three tones or DS or even both in some cases
(Hyman 1986).

Shilluk Phonology

In an attempt to discriminate between M tone and a downstepped H (!H), Hyman (1986:128) has contrasted the characteristics of each one. No one characteristic should be taken as the deciding factor. However, taken together, we should be able to reach a consensus.

Hyman gives five characteristics. Only four will be discussed since the last point, the frequency of a fourth tone, is irrelevant for Shilluk which has only three pitch levels.

After pause. The first point Hyman makes is that M tone is expected at the beginning of an utterance. !H is not expected to contrast with H utterance-initial.

We turn to the data for Shilluk. H, M, and L tones contrast after pause (utterance-initial).

(90) ábámàc   'type of bird'
      àcyén   'curse'
      ādígáwɔ̀w   'sunset'
      ādṳ̀:l   'circular things'
      gɔ̄:lɔ́   'hook'
      wā:c   'books'
      by ēr   'roots'

We see that H, M, and L tones contrast before pause. Further, the M tone may be followed by H, M, or L or may occur by itself as in the last three words in (90). Thus, we have the answer to one question concerning interpreting the third tone as M rather than !H.

Ceiling. In Hyman's second point, M tone should allow a higher pitch on a following H tone whereas !H would lower the subsequent H to the same level. We know from (85) that H, M, and L may be followed by H across a morpheme boundary. Below we have further examples within single words.

(91) átṵ́dɔ́   'duck'   [‾ˋ‾]
      ókɔ̰̄t:ị̄   'grainbins'   [‾ˋ‑]
      ágā̰k:ị̀   'ravens'   [‾ˋ˯]

H, M, and L all contrast after HM. There is no ceiling set by the M tone, and so we have one more point in favor of M over !H.

Limitations. In his third criterion, Hyman indicates that M tone is expected to be local, "affecting only a TBU [tone bearing unit] or perhaps a single tonal autosegment." The !H is expected to be unbounded and can

50   Phonetics, Phonemics, and Postlexical Phonology

affect not only all the subsequent H's but any other tone as well. By way
of example, Hyman says the second L in the sequence L-H-!H-L is lower than
the first L. However, if the sequence were L-H-M-L, the two L's would be
the same.

Shilluk has very few four-syllable words, so we need to turn to phrases
and sentences. As these rules are general phonological rules, any effects
should be present over a longer string.

(92)   [- _ _ ⁻ ⁻ - _   - ⁻ ⁻ _ _ ⌐]
      ka jiy pa-ani ri̠:ŋa wɔk / / ki lwak ki jɔk mɔ gi:r
      And people of this village ran out from the barn with many men.

All L tones in this sentence are on the same pitch. There is no sign of
lowering even by means of downdrift.

We see, then, that the sequence L-H-M-L $[\bar{\ }\bar{\ }\bar{\ }]$ is what we get in Shilluk
rather than L-H-!H-L $[\bar{\ }\bar{\ }\bar{\ }]$. This adds a third argument for interpreting our
third pitch as a M tone.

Cumulative effect. In Hyman's fourth (and our final) point, M tone is not
expected to be CUMULATIVE. In principle, an indefinite series of !H's would
be possible. However, lowering to M followed by a second M would result
in the two tones being at the same level. Several examples are given below
showing various environments.

(93)   [⁻ - - - ⁻ _ _ _ - ⁻]
      kipaŋɔ arɔt o̠tɔn̠ɔ ki yo:?
      Why were the children attacked on the road?

(94)   [- ⁻ — - ⌐]
      ka omi̠a ɲel dwɔ̠ŋ
      and my elder brother

(95)   [- _ _ ⁻ ⁻ - - _]
      ka jiy pa-ani ri̠:ŋa wɔk.
      And people of this village ran out.

Two to three M tones may occur together and remain at the same level.
Also, the M tones may be preceded by either H or L. There is no compelling
evidence to say that sequences of !H are present. Thus, we have the fourth
to adduce as evidence that our third pitch is M tone rather than !H.

Shilluk Phonology

Sequences. Now that we have decided that there are three underlying level tones in Shilluk, we may consider the rest of the facts about the tone. Not only are there three level tones, but nearly every possible sequence of tones is found on the root. Examples of level tones are repeated along with words having sequences of tones. A combination of tones marked with a ligature, such as HL, indicates a contour tone.

(96)

H	*bák*	'garden'
M	*bāɲ*	'cow with drooping horns'
L	*bàk*	'guess!'
H͡L	*bâ̰ŋ*	'servant'
M͡L	*bwɔ̰̄c*	'barren person'
M͡H	*bāt*	'arm'
L͡H	*byḛ̌c*	'cow with horns straight out'

The only sequence that is not found on the root (which is necessarily monosyllabic) is LM. The matrix below shows the tone patterns on roots. The H-H combination simply means a level H. This is necessary in order to construct a complete matrix.

(97)

	H	M	L
H	X	X	X
M	X	X	X
L	X		X

If we move on to the prefix + root words, we see that many of the tone sequences are possible.

(98)

HH͡L	*ábîp*	'measles'
HL͡H	*ámǎl*	'camels' (R = rare)
LH͡L	*àbôn*	'pastor'
LL͡H	*a̰yák*	'sleeping cover'

Once again, a matrix may help us to see the general patterns in the language.

52   Phonetics, Phonemics, and Postlexical Phonology

(99)   Root tones

		H	M	L	HL	LH
Prefix	H	x	x	x	x	x
tones	M			x		
	L	x	x	x	x	x

At this point we are describing sequences of tones across a morpheme
boundary, namely, the nominalizer prefix and the root. The new matrix is
quite different from (83).

There are a total of eleven tone patterns represented in the prefix +
root words. We notice that there is a limited use of M tone on a prefix.
There is also a noticeable absence of M tones within the contour tones on
the root. There are no MH, HM or LM contours on the root even though MH
and HM are present on monosyllabic roots.

We come now to an interesting situation. Words which consist of root
+ suffix, seem to have a restricted distribution of plurals: HM, HLL, LL.
These patterns are seen in the plural words in (100).

(100) HM   gám:ī   'midwives'
       HLL   ɲwêl:ì   'earthworms'
       LL   tṳk:ì   'rocks of mud'

If we compare the tone patterns of singular words (101) with the same
root + suffix SHAPE, we see quite a difference in the number of options.

(101) HH   dɔ́:rɔ́   'axe'
       HMM   bá̠:ɲɔ̄   'grasshopper'
       HL   bṳ́dɔ̀   'zucchini'
       MM   dō:dɔ̄   'tumble bug'
       MLL   bṳ̄gɔ̀   'cow with dead calf'
       LL   dwa̠:lɔ̀ 'fat'
       LH   byȅ:lɔ́ 'stalk of millet'

In chapter 4, we discuss a process whereby plurals are derived. For the
purpose of the present discussion, we will simply say that the plural suffix
-i is moved into the root along with its tone. Technically, it then becomes
a one-syllable word. However, if we include these derived plurals in our
tone data for two-syllable words, we see that the tone patterns on plurals
are not as restricted as was previously assumed. Consider the following.

Shilluk Phonology   53

(102) H   kwé:r   'small lizards' (R)
       HM   bâ̰:c   'outer layers of plant'
              gám:ḭ   'midwives'
       HL   bâ̰:ɲ   'grasshoppers'
              ɲwêl:ì   'earthworms'
       M   wā̰:c   'books'
       ML   bà̰:t   'arms'
       L   dà:t   'hooves'
              t ṵ̀k:ḭ   'rocks of mud'
       LH   bwɔ̰:c   'barren people'

Before returning to our analysis, we will look at the three-syllable words.
In our earlier discussion, we had only the level tones. We saw very few
tone possibilites of level tones on three-syllable words. In fact, there are
quite a few more possibilities, but we must include tone sequences in order
to see them. The same assumption is made here with regard to derived
plurals, as was just discussed in the previous section.

(103) HHĤLH   átṵ̂dɔ́   'duck'
       HHĤLL   átê:gɔ̀   'goat '
       HHĤMM   álwê:dɔ́   'crab'
       HLL   ácṵ̀ŋɔ̀   'black mound termite'
       HHĤML   ágāk:ḭ   'ravens'
       ML   ādṵ̀:l   'circular things'
       LMH   àbā:rɔ́   'fencing grass'
       LHĤLL   àbṵ̂rɔ̀   'reedbuck'
       LLL   àdṵ̀dɔ̀   'large sieve'
       LH   ɲìbɔ́:w   'white calves' (R)
       LLĤH   dìdṵ̂:k   'dark grey bulls'

It seems that level tones are the exception rather than the rule on
three-syllable words in Shilluk. If the hypothesis is true, that western
Nilotic languages are moving from multi-syllable words to mono-syllable
words, then we can make some conjectures as to the tone. Goldsmith
(1976) discusses the phenomenon of TONE STABILITY. He argues that the
tone melody is independently maintained even when the syllable structure
of the word changes. The tone which is left without a tone bearing unit
(TBU), does not delete, but simply moves to the next available location.
    Evidence from Shilluk seems to confirm this principle of tone stability.
As segments in Shilluk words were dropped, the tone shifted to the root.
In three-syllable words, we see the resultant bunching of tones. However,
as words got shorter still, it became necessary to utilize M tone which is

distinct, rather than the ₁H which it may have been. This was necessary in order to preserve the structure and semantic information. As words became even shorter, i.e., mono-syllables, all three level tones and most of the possible tone sequences had to be used in order to distinguish the segments. Hence, there is a greater number of sequences allowed on monosyllabic roots than on two-syllable words. I offer these remarks only tentatively. Obviously, further research into the historical reconstruction is needed to confirm such an hypothesis. However, such a study is not within the scope of this paper. I leave this idea for the present and continue the analysis of tone.

The remainder of our discussion of tone will focus on three areas: a) a further argument against spreading and tone assimilation based on the data just presented; b) the different tone patterns permitted between singular and plural nouns; and finally, c) the principles for relating the autosegmental tier with the timing tier.

Spreading. Having added tone sequences to our data base, we need to look at tone spreading. According to Goldsmith (1976), automatic spreading is not the result of a phonological rule. Instead, spreading is the result of the geometry of the autosegmental representation as well as the WELL-FORMEDNESS CONDITION.

We have an example of spreading provided by Schuh (1978) from Ngizim and Duwai (Chadic languages). According to Schuh, spreading is the "extension of a *single* tone beyond its original domain" (230). He gives the following rule: LO HI HI → LO LO HI. This could be interpreted in autosegmental terms (recalling that Schuh's paper was written prior to Goldsmith).

(104)

Looking for such a process in Shilluk, we find that it could be reckoned as a process in some words, but could not begin to account for all of the data. Consider the following data.

(105) LLH   *àyĕk*   'sleeping cover'
      LLH   *òtặŋ*   'black animals'

Shilluk Phonology   55

but

(106) LH   àḍút   'stinger of bee'
             ɲìbɔ́:w   'white calves'
       LM   àbɔ́y   'rotten fish'

In (105), we could posit a process of spreading. However, it would be difficult to block that spreading in (106). In fact, words like those of (105) occur more frequently, and are obviously not subject to spreading. Further evidence against spreading is seen in (107).

(107)   + ání

       gâr   gá̰:rání   'northern Shilluk person'

In (107), we see a HL contour on the citation form. When the marker -ání 'this' is added, the L tone from the root fails to spread to the next syllable. Not only that, the L tone is lost altogether. Even though the vowel is doubled in the inflected form, the L tone still does not surface. These data offer yet another argument against the idea that spreading be used to account for the M tone in Shilluk.

Earlier, in §2.6, we saw that Shilluk offers an argument for tone stability. Yet, in the example just presented, we see the loss of a tone, even where there is no loss of a tone-bearing unit. Rather than assuming this situation to represent a case militating against tone stability, it seems more likely that there is a tone delinking rule in operation. This tone delinking rule is discussed in §5.1. The point being made by Goldsmith in relation to tone stability is that the tiers of tone and segment are somewhat independent. The evidence from Shilluk readily supports that premise. In this case, tone is delinked while the segment remains intact. In the case of the plural derivation, the tone is retained even with the loss of the tone bearing unit. Thus, the tonal tier and segmental tier are able to function independently.

Assimilation revisited. Although the status of the three tones in Shilluk has been established, there is one further point which can be made on the subject. In light of the tone sequences in Shilluk, let us look again at assimilation. We may simply assume that the tone sequence [MH] is an underlying /LH/ and [ML] is /HL/.

(108) bāt   'arm'   /LH/   [‾ ‾]
       cyə̰̂w 'porcupines' /HL/   [‾ _]

56 Phonetics, Phonemics, and Postlexical Phonology

However, we have some problem distinguishing these words from those which are realized on the surface as [LH] and [HL].

(109) kŭl   'pigs'   [╯]
      bân̰   'servant'   [╲]

We would have further difficulties accounting for M tone in words which have no other surface tones nearby as in MM.

(110) gɔ̄:lɔ̄ 'hook'   [- -]

Therefore, we conclude again that there is M tone in Shilluk. In addition, all sequences of the three tones may occur with only a minimum of restriction. These restrictions are discussed below.

Singular and plural tones. We come to another interesting aspect of Shilluk tonology. It seems that the number category of the noun has some influence on the tone. As mentioned earlier, the possession marker on a singular noun regularly has M tone whereas the same marker on a plural noun has H tone. However, the influence of number category on tone seems to be even more far reaching. There are certain tone patterns which *never* occur with plural words and other tone patterns which *never* occur on singular words. The majority of patterns can occur on both. The various restrictions will be given below with examples.

We begin with one-syllable words since they have the fewest restrictions. Actually, there seems to be only one restriction; namely, that M̄H occurs only with singular roots and H̄M occurs only with plural roots.

(111)   MONOSYLLABIC ROOT TONE RESTRICTION (MRTR)

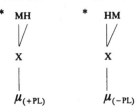

These tones are restricted by the number category of the noun. The examples below show what is permissible.

(112) M̄H b̄at   'arm'
      H S dyēn̰   'baby baskets'

Shilluk Phonology

There are several more restrictions on words with prefix and root. Looking again at the matrix given in (99), we add the information relevant to the singular and plural occurrences.

(113)   Root tones
                    H   M   L   HL   LH
         Prefix H SG   SG/PL SG/PL SG/PL   PL
         tones   M   PL
                 L SG   SG/PL SG/PL   SG   SG/PL

The most general restriction is that the root tone must be L when there is M tone on the prefix of a plural noun (114). An example of this tone pattern is *ādwɔ̄k* 'gum trees'.

(114) L ROOT TONE RESTRICTION

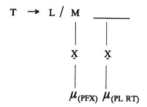

There is one other PLURAL ONLY tone pattern in two-syllable words, H tone on the prefix and LH on the root.

(115) PLURAL TONE RESTRICTION

NM → (+PL) / H   LH
              | |/
              x   x
              | |
             μ(PFX) μ(__RT)

If the tone pattern of a noun is HLH, its number category must be plural; singular nouns may not have this tone pattern. An example is *ámăl* 'camels'.

There are three tone patterns which occur only with singular words.

(116) H prefix + H root
       L prefix + H root
       L prefix + HL root

(117) SINGULAR TONE RESTRICTIONS

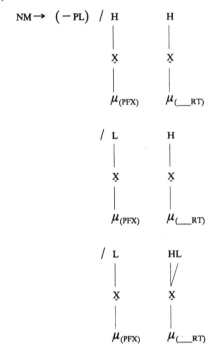

In nouns with prefix + root the following tone patterns occur only with singular (or [−PL]) words: HH, LH, LHÎ.

(118) álám   'dragnet'
     àḍụ́ṭ   'stinger of bee'
     àbôn   'pastor'

There are no number restrictions for root + suffix words like the restrictions on the previous words. The two sequences M on the root + H on the suffix and L on the root + M on the suffix, however, do not occur. The suffix in question is the number suffix (NM) which indicates the singular or plural status of the root. The restriction does not apply when adding a morpheme such as the possession marker.

The first non-occurrence is slightly suspicious. Looking at three-syllable words, we find a sequence of LMH. This word gives us M on the root followed by H tone on the NM suffix. We suggest that there is no restriction on this sequence, but that its failure to occur may simply be the result of insufficient data.

Shilluk Phonology

The other sequence, L+M seems to be a genuine restriction. The rule states that the tone sequence LM may not occur within the noun stem (119).

(119) ROOT + SUFFIX TONE RESTRICTION

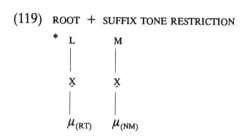

In conclusion, we have seen that certain tonal sequences are restricted and that certain sequences may occur only with singular or plural roots, the remainder occurring with either. No explanation is offered for this interrelationship except to suggest that with such a large number of tonal options, there needs to be a limitation somewhere.

2.7. Underspecification and tone

So far in the analysis, Shilluk is shown to have three level tones. But what is the best way to define the distinctive features with regard to tone? Hyman (1986) has reviewed various recent proposals for handling three and four tones in terms of feature systems. He seems to agree with Pulleyblank (1983) that M tone is unmarked. In Hyman's interpretation (1986:115), M tone is the "untoned" tone bearing unit while the "h" means "go up one step" and the "l" says "to go down one step." Hyman then goes on to suggest multiple tiers for tone in his analysis.

I have chosen, however, to utilize Archangeli's theory of underspecification whenever possible with respect to segments. Since Pulleyblank's analysis (1986) also incorporates underspecification, I am using his approach to tonal analysis.

Pulleyblank (1983, 1986) argued that in a three-tone system, M tone is the unmarked or underspecified tone. Adopting that position for Shilluk results in the following underspecified tone matrix.

(120)   H   M   L
   High +
   Low   +

60 Phonetics, Phonemics, and Postlexical Phonology

The redundancy rules would include those in (121).

(121) [+HI] → [−LO] DR
      [+LO] → [−HI] DR
      [ ] → [−HI] CR
      [ ] → [−LO] CR

The fully specified tone matrix is in (122).

(122)

	H	M	L
High	+	−	−
Low	−	−	+

2.8. Principles of association

In this final section, we will begin to consider how the tonal and segmental tiers are associated. First, let us consider the OBLIGATORY CONTOUR PRINCIPLE (OCP) proposed originally by Leben (1971). The OCP excludes the possibility of adjacent autosegments having the same value. In later works, however, many problems have arisen over OCP as a universal principle. Van der Hulst and Smith (1985a:16) suggest that OCP is reduced to a principle "that *allows* one to collapse identical autosegments" unless there is some reason for them to be kept separate. In Shilluk, there do not appear to be any counterexamples to the OCP with respect to tone. Once we have established the sequences allowed in the autosegmental tier, we can relate the tonal tier, in this case, to the segmental tier by means of association lines. The conditions for association were given in chapter 1 and will not be repeated here.

Shilluk seems to make use of all three of these associating conventions. First, we see a one-to-one correspondence in a word like *bák* 'garden'. The H tone is associated with the word. The association line is drawn from the tone to the tone-bearing unit which, in Shilluk, is always a vowel.

(123) H   H
              |

/bak/ → [bak]

When there are more tones than tone-bearing units, the remaining tone is associated to the nearest tone-bearing unit. In the case of *bâŋ* 'servant' we are able to account for the tones in the following way.

Shilluk Phonology   61

(124)   HL   HL   HL

/baŋ/ → baŋ → [baŋ]

The HL is assigned to the word. The first tone is associated with the tone-bearing unit and the remaining L tone is associated by dumping it on to the same tone-bearing unit.

In the event that there are more segments than tones, spreading occurs as in (125).

(125)   L   L   L

/tukki/ → tukki → [tuk:i]

The L tone is assigned to the word. The first association is made to the leftmost tone-bearing unit. With no further tones, the tone spreads to the rest of the word.

What has been presented is only a basic overview of the tone analysis. It is not intended to deal with all of the problems of Shilluk tone. Those problems and their solutions are covered in more detail in chapter 5.

2.9. Conclusion

We have investigated various ways in which three pitch levels might be accounted for by means of two underlying tones (H and L). We saw that assimilation, dissimilation, and upstep failed to adequately account for the data. Finally, when comparing the characteristics of M tone with ¡H, we found that all four points agreed that Shilluk has M tone rather than ¡H. For the remainder of this paper, we will assume three level tones: H M L.

We also saw the large variety of tone sequences allowed in Shilluk. There are some restrictions on tone sequences related to the number category which were listed and discussed.

Finally, the procedures for associating the autosegmental tier to the timing tier were discussed.

Abbreviations

DHSR	(71)	DIPHTHONG HIGH SPREADING RULE
GVC	(58)	GLIDE AND VOWEL CONSTRAINT
IAR	(68)	INTERVOCALIC ASPIRATION RULE
ICS	(56)	INITIAL CONSONANT SEQUENCE
ICSC	(57)	INITIAL CONSONANT SEQUENCE CONSTRAINT
IGCSC	(67)	INITIAL GEMINATE CONSONANT SEQUENCE CONSTRAINT
OHSR	(72)	OFF-GLIDE HIGH SPREADING RULE
PSR	(60)	PHONETIC SHORTENING RULE
SFD	(63)	SYLLABLE-FINAL DEVOICING
TR	(59)	TENSING RULE
TVR	(66)	TENSE-VOICING RULE

3
Representation of Lexical Items

Among the tantalizing experiences in the world of linguistic investigation, the study of Shilluk must surely rank high. The apparent absence of methodical "grammar" and the relative ease with which beginners can pick up a smattering, are factors which at first invite and then bemuse the serious investigator (Tucker 1955:421).

3.1. Syntax

We begin our discussion of Shilluk morphology with a brief synopsis of the syntax of nouns and verbs. This section has been included in order to establish the syntactic terminology which will be used throughout the remainder of this paper and is not intended to be a definitive statement of Shilluk syntax.

After defining our terminology, we will turn to a consideration of the typical components of a word and will examine the prefixes and suffixes and their role in the word. Compound words will also be discussed briefly before moving on to the representation of lexical items.

Nominal system. Shilluk nouns do not divide simply into singulars and plurals. Instead, it is more appropriate to speak of morphologically marked and unmarked forms. These marked and unmarked forms do not correlate with semantic singular and plural. Instead, there needs to be a category which is neutral to number in which the unmarked words are placed. In (126) and (127) the neutral forms are semantically singular, while in (128) and (129), the neutral forms are collective and plural respectively.

64	Representation of Lexical Items

Neutral   Plural

(126) *yép*   'tail'   *yè:p*   'tails'
(127) *ɲâŋ*   'crocodile'   *ɲáŋ:ī*   'crocodiles'

Singulative   Neutral

(128) *byè:lɔ́*   'a piece of millet'   *byél*   'millet'
(129) *wà:rɔ̀*   'shoe'   *wâr*   'shoes'

For contrast, look at the marked forms of these words (plural in (126) and (127) and singulative in (128) and (129)). The marked forms generally have either the -ɔ suffix which indicates that it is singular or an -i suffix or a long root vowel[10] indicating that it is plural.

In order to complete the system, we need to look at a third set of words which has a singulative and a plural but no neutral form. In other words, both forms are morphologically marked.

Singulative   Plural

(130) *àdè:rɔ̀*   'donkey'   *àdè:r*   'donkeys'
(131) *ácùŋɔ̀*   'type of termite'   *ácùŋ:ì*   'type of termites'

With these examples, we have seen that there are three noun sets in Shilluk. The first set has a neutral form which happens to be singular while the morphologically marked form is a plural. In the second set, the neutral form seems to function semantically as a collective or plural and has a singulative counterpart. The third set of words, which follows many of the rules given for the second set, have number markers on both forms. The two members of this third set are singulative and plural; no neutral form is found.

For the purposes of this paper, the singular neutral form will be termed SINGULAR (SG). The plural words in the neutral category will be called COLLECTIVES (COLL). In this way, they will not be confused with each other (which would happen if only the morphologically based label neutral was used). They will also be distinct from their marked counterparts, SINGULATIVE (SGLT) and PLURAL (PL).

---

[10]A more complete explanation of the long vowel appears in chapter 4.

Shilluk Phonology

(132)		Marked	Unmarked	Marked
Set 1		————	neutral (SG)	plural
Set 2		singulative	neutral (COLL)	————
Set 3		singulative	————	plural

It is worth noting that there is no subject/verb agreement which would signal singular or plural. Furthermore, only indefinite nouns are indicated by *ki*, which can translate as 'a' or 'some' depending on the noun which follows it. Definiteness is not indicated overtly; it is the default value. Singularity or plurality can only be expressed syntactically if a quantifier is used or if the noun is modified by one of the few adjectives which happen to have a singular or plural form. Most adjectives have only one form which can be used with either singular or plural nouns.

There is further evidence for setting up the three noun sets described above. Consider nouns which are in a genitive relationship with another noun or a determiner.

(133) Set 1	SG	PL	
bul̪ gɔn	*bul̪:i gɔn*	'his drum/s'
kwey wɔn	*kwey:i wɔn*	'our grandfather/s'
ɔd gwet	*ɔt:i gwe:t*	'house/s of writing'

(134) Set 2	SGLT	COLL	
wi:ni ɗɔ ŋu:	*wi:n ɗɔ ŋu:*	'lion's whisker/s'
ye̪:yi ŋu:	*ye̪:y ŋu:*	'lion's hair/s'
wiyi gen	*we̪:k gen*	'their father/s'

(135) Set 3	SGLT	PL	
apwɔɲ:i gɔn	*apwɔc:i gɔn*	'his rabbit/s'

The relative order for the genitive construction is Possessed (PSD) + Possessor (PSR). Note that in Set 1, the plural form has PSD + i + PSR. In Set 2, the SGLT form has the same PSD + i + PSR construction. When we look at Set 3, we see that *both* forms have the -i possession marker. Notice further that in the SG and COLL (i.e., unmarked) forms there is no such possession marker.

Since the -i possessive marker may occur with what are semantically singular as well as plural forms, and in some cases with both, we would be at a loss as to how to predict its distribution. However, if we operate with the dichotomy of morphologically unmarked versus marked forms, we can readily state that the -i possessive marker occurs with non-neutral forms.

Thus, we see that there is independent confirmation that our marked/unmarked dichotomy is useful.

Verbal system. Both Kohnen (1933) and Tucker (1955) have attempted to classify Shilluk verbs. Their observations and explanations of the data give an understanding of the issues at hand. No attempt is made to prove one view or the other but to simply define terms which more adequately reflect the syntactic usage of the various verb forms found in the data base.

Kohnen's (1933) diagram of the classification of Shilluk is shown in (136).

(136)
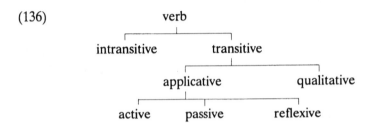

He divides verbs into transitive and intransitive, and though he does not define intransitive, he does give examples such as *ya catho* 'I walk'.

Kohnen then divides transitive into applicative or qualitative. According to Kohnen, an applicative form "rules a direct, determinate, actual, present object." The qualitative form "has no direct, determinate accusative object" (1933:123). He cites the examples in (137).

(137) ya thala riŋani   'I cook this meat'   (APP)
       ya tado   'I am cooking'   (QUAL)

Kohnen further subdivides the applicative into active, passive and reflexive. I have not investigated the reflexive; so it will receive no further attention.

Tucker (1955) does not diagram his system *per se*, but from his description it would probably be as follows:

(138)
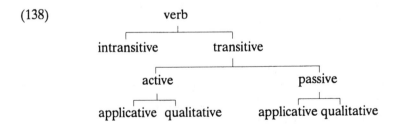

Shilluk Phonology   67

He divides transitive verb forms into active and passive.

(139) yá gɔca gwòk   'I am beating the dog'   (ACT)
       yán a gɔ̂c (yì ŋati)   'I am being beaten   (PASS)
                             (by someone)' (p. 432)

He then treats applicative and qualitative as subdivisions under each
voice. The applicative has a specific object (for active) or agent (for
passive) which is mentioned or understood, as in the examples above. A
qualitative form refers to a verb "without reference to an object or noun
agent, or applying to it only in a general sense" (p. 432). Further, he says
that an intransitive verb "may be said to conjugate as a Qualitative verb."
This raises the question of how he would distinguish between intransitive
and qualitative. Tucker does not address that question. Some further
examples are in (140).

(140) yâ· gòcò   'I am beating'   (ACT)
       yâ· gɔ̀ɔ̀jɔ̀   'I am being beaten'   (PASS)
       ya kɛdhɔ   'I go'   (INTR)
       ya dɔɔgɔ   'I return'   (INTR) (pp. 432, 447, 449)

It is interesting to note that the passive is considered to be more
common than the active. According to Tucker, the passive is "on the whole
more in use than 'the Active' in everyday conversation" (432). Kohnen
(1933) makes a similar comment, "Shilluks preferably make use of the
passive voice of the transitive verbs, particularly in the *future* and *past*
tenses indicative and in the conditional mood" (133). Finally,
Westermann's comment (1912:78) expresses an honest view of the difficulty in even *hearing* the changes between the voices when he says,

> Most foreigners have considerable difficulties in distinguishing
> the active voice from the passive, the difference between both
> lying in most cases solely in the intonation . . . the natives prefer
> to speak in the passive voice; therefore, the foreigner can best
> avoid misunderstandings by using the passive voice as much as
> possible and by supposing that what a native tells him, to be
> passive, and not active.

Okoth-Okombo (1982) states that in Dholuo, the intransitive verb has
two forms. One form refers to action with no logical object as in *nind-* 'to
sleep'. This form is called INTRANSITIVE. The second form, QUALITATIVE, is

an action in which the object is understood but not expressed. An example of a qualitative verb is *meṭo* 'to drink'.

For Turkana, Dimmendaal (1983) reports that an intransitive verb has one noun phrase as the subject with a nominative case marking. Transitive verbs have both a subject and a direct object. The third type of verb is impersonal active from which a subject NP is absent. This third type probably corresponds to the passive in Shilluk. He does not describe anything that seems to correspond to the qualitative verbs in Shilluk as discussed by both Kohnen and Tucker.

Reh (1986) discusses similar phenomena in Anywak. She terms the transitive verb an ACTION PROCESS verb form. This term implies that both agent and patient participants are present. The qualitative form is called a PATIENT DELETING derivation. In this case, the verb is an action verb which no longer allows a patient participant.

Constituent order. So far, none of the descriptions of Shilluk syntax seems to have dealt adequately with the data. Constituent order is such an intrinsic part of the verb system that when one tries to separate constituent order from the verb type, an incredible amount of confusion results. Unfortunately, keeping them together can be equally confusing.

There are certain transitive verb forms, Form A and Form B, which cannot be defined within current syntactic terms. The information presented here attempts to clarify the nature of these forms.

We will begin with constituent order. An ACTIVE clause will consist of the following functions: subject (s) + verb (vB) + complement (cMP). The s is expressed by an agent (A) and the cMP may be expressed by a patient (P), benefactive (BEN), instrument (INST), or location (LOC). The passive has the same set of constituents s + vB + cMP. But, the s slot is expressed by a patient and the cMP slot by an agent.

(141)

S	VB	CMP	ACTIVE
A		P	

S	VB	CMP	PASSIVE
P		A	

Examples of each constituent order type are given in (142) and (143).

Shilluk Phonology   69

(142) ACTIVE   S/A   VB   CMP/P
                ya   ṭal:a   kwan
                1ps   cook   porridge
                I cook the porridge.

                S/A   VB   CMP/P
                ja:l   dwɔŋ   yep:a   ḍɔ ɔt
                male   big   open   mouth house
                The man opens the door.

(143) PASSIVE   S/P   VB   CMP/A
                kwan   ṭal   yi   yan
                porridge cook   by   1ps
                The porridge is cooked by me.

                S/P   VB   CMP/A
                ḍɔ   ɔt   yep   yi   ja:l   dwɔŋ
                mouth   house   open   by   male   big
                The door is opened by the man.

In addition to the active and passive orders, there is also a VB + S + CMP
order. This verb-initial order is never discussed by Kohnen (1933) or
Tucker (1955), nor by Tucker and Bryan (1966). However, it occurs most
frequently in texts and its neglect may be due to its being perceived as an
incomplete passive. We shall refer to this order as the NARRATIVE CON-
STITUENT ORDER. The verb is followed by the subject expressing the agent
and then the complement expressing the patient. Both active and passive
voices are found with the verb-initial narrative clauses.

(144) ACTIVE   VB   S/A   CMP/P
                ayo:t   wɔ   jiy   be:n
                PST^find 1p   people   all
                We found all the people sitting.

                VB   S/A   CMP/P
                abwɔk   jiy   keti   gen
                PST^fear people   REFL   3p
                The people became afraid.

70   Representation of Lexical Items

(145) PASSIVE   VB   S/P   CMP/LOC
                adɔːk   *wɔn*   *pa*   *wɔn*
                PST^return   1p   village   1p
                We were returned to our village.

                VB   S/P   CMP/A
                acyẹtːi   *gen*   *yị*   *wɔn*
                PST^chase   3p   by   1p
                They were chased by us.

                VB   S/P   CMP/A
                ajoːk   *wɔn*   *yị*   *jɔk*   *pa*   *ani*
                PST^convince   1p   by   men   village   this
                We were convinced by the men of this village.

Careful examination of this VSCMP order reveals some important information. First, the S slot is contiguous to the verb. This is also true of the
SVCMP order. Secondly, the S has no morphological marking (in particular,
there is no adposition).

The examples of passives (145) show the S/P determiner in the objective
case. (The objective case is indicated in Shilluk by the addition of -*n* to the
pronoun.)

Now we come to yet another ordering of constituents: VCMPCMP. Examples are shown in (146)–(148). In this order, there is no S. Because S
cannot have an adposition, the *yị* + NP found in the examples precludes
this structure having S status, even though it is contiguous to the verb. The
second CMP cannot have S status because it is not contiguous to the verb.
Therefore, we have a sentence without a subject in which we have CMP/A
and CMP/P as in (148).

(146) VB   CMP/A   CMP/INST
      abẹːn   *yị*   *jaːl*   *mekɔ*   *ki*   *tɔŋ*
      PST^come   by   man   other   with   spear
      Another man came with a spear.

(147)   VB   CMP/A
      ka   *bẹːn*   *yị*   *en*
      when   come   by   3s
      When he came ...

(148)   VB   CMP/A   CMP/P
      ka   *ɲi-makːi*   *yị ŋuː* *ki*   *laːy*
      when   HAB-catch   by lion   INDEF   animal
      When an animal was caught by the lion ...

Shilluk Phonology 71

Thus, we can contrast the SVCMP, VSCMP and VCMPCMP orders. The s in the VSCMP order has no morphological marking and is contiguous to the verb. The s in the SVCMP order meets the same criteria. By contrast, however, the constituent immediately following the verb in the VCMPCMP order has an adposition. The third constituent is not contiguous to the verb and so cannot be assigned s status.

If we assume that the analysis so far is correct, then there should be some factor which would suggest when one construction should be used instead of the other. In studying several different types of narratives, there seems to be evidence to suggest that the VCMPCMP order is more commonly used in narratives which are told by a third party. The VSCMP pattern occurs in narratives in which the narrator is a participant in the action. More research is needed to confirm this hypothesis, so, for the present, I am suggesting that there are two verb-initial constituent orders (149).

(149)
$$\underline{\text{V} \quad \text{CMP} \quad \text{CMP}} \qquad \text{narrator} \neq \text{participant}$$
$$\phantom{\text{V} \quad} \text{A} \qquad \text{X}$$

and

$$\underline{\text{V} \quad \text{S} \quad \text{CMP}} \qquad \text{narrator} = \text{participant}$$
$$\phantom{\text{V} \quad} \text{A} \qquad \text{X}$$

In the first order, VCMPCMP, the first CMP slot is filled by an agent, who is not the narrator. This slot must be filled by a yi + NP. The second CMP may be filled by patient or location. An x is used to show that more than one type of semantic role may be expressed in this position.

The second verb-initial order, VSCMP, assumes the narrator to be a participant. The s as agent follows the verb and may be filled by any semantically appropriate NP. There is no morphological marking. The s slot *always* follows the verb. Any other NP must be considered a complement.

The VSCMP order operates with both active and passive voices whereas the VCMPCMP order seems to only include the active. Thus, in the VSCMP order, the s may express the agent in the active voice or the patient in the passive voice. The CMP slot will express the patient in the active voice and the agent in the passive voice. There may be other fillers, but there is insufficient data to draw further conclusions at this time.

So far, we have three constituent orders: SVCMP, VSCMP and VCMPCMP. The active and passive voices can be found in the SVCMP and VSCMP. The VCMPCMP can only have the active voice. A diagram of this information is shown in (150).

(150)

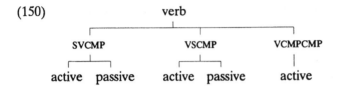

Now that we have established the constituent order of Shilluk, we need to look briefly at the transitive and intransitive verbs. On the clause level, the surface forms of transitive and intransitive verbs are identical—(151a) and (152a).

(151a) INTRANSITIVE   S/A VB   CMP/LOC
ka jiy reŋ:a[11] pa ani
and people PST^run village that
And people ran to that village.

(152a) TRANSITIVE   S/A VB   CMP/P
ŋu: ca:ma la:y
lion eat animals
The lion eats the animals.

In SVCMP order, the -a is obligatory if there is a CMP slot. In the examples, the CMP may be expressed by either a locative or a patient. The only way to identify an intransitive verb by some means other than semantic content is to find the active verb form without a CMP. In such a case, the intransitive verb root will be IDENTICAL to the root of that verb with a CMP. If the verb is transitive, there will be a difference in the stem between the +CMP and −CMP forms.

(151b) INTRANSITIVE S/A VB
ka jiy reŋ
and people run
And the people run.

(152b) TRANSITIVE S/A VB
ŋu: cya:m
lion eat
The lion eats.

---

[11]These words [reŋ:] and [reŋ] are the same underlyingly. A syllable structure rule shortens the geminate consonant word-finally.

Shilluk Phonology 73

We see that the intransitive verb *reŋ* has the same root whether or not a locative is mentioned. However, with the transitive root, *ca:m* with the patient and *cya:m* without the patient are seen. Often the distinction in these forms lies in the initial consonant and the [EX] feature of the vowel.

We have now seen one of the paradoxes in Shilluk syntax; transitive and intransitive verbs are distinctly different on one hand, but behave very similarly on the other. To handle them separately ignores the obviously large overlap. To deal with them together could imply that they are identical. In order to avoid these extremes, I shall refer to a category of TRANSITIVE (in small caps). This TRANSITIVE category will include both transitive and intransitive verbs, but will hopefully signal to the reader that I am using this term in a broader sense than it normally conveys. Thus, I can describe the generalities of the system without unnecessary redundancy.

In summary, there are three constituent orders: SVCMP, VSCMP, and VCMPCMP. The SVCMP and VSCMP may have active or passive voices. Only the active voice may apply to the VCMPCMP order. The s expresses the agent in the active while in the passive the s expresses the patient.

In the VSCMP order, the narrator is a participant in the event. This consideration employs a morphologically unmarked NP to act as S/A. In other third party discourses, the agent in the post-verb position is always indicated by *yi* + NP. The second constituent cannot be s in this case, since s cannot be filled by an adposition phrase in Shilluk. Thus, we have the VCMPCMP type of narrative.

Finally, we are using TRANSITIVE to indicate both transitive and intransitive verbs in order to capture the generalizations between these two types of verbs.

Complements. Now we come to one of the most intriguing aspects of Shilluk syntax: complements. This area of the verb system seems, at face value, to be fairly straightforward. The language learner soon catches onto the gist of things, even though it is difficult to express in words. Kohnen called these verb forms QUALITATIVE, probably for lack of any other more enlightening terminology. His lead has been faithfully followed by others, until recently. In an earlier version of this paper, I considered using the terms complement versus non-complement to describe the situation. However, it soon became apparent that this terminology did not adequately account for the data. The summary given here is far from satisfactory. However, I shall try to present the data as it is currently understood and attach some label to it. At least then it can be discussed, even if it is not fully understood.

Let us begin with the active side of the SVCMP order. The CMP in this case is marked by *-a* suffixed to the verb as in (153).

74   Representation of Lexical Items

(153)   S/A   VB   CMP/P

ḍeṇ   dwɔŋ   aṭal:a   riŋɔ

female   big   PST^cook   meat

The woman cooked the meat.

In this sentence, the CMP is expressed by a patient. However, if the CMP were not included, the result would not be *ḍeṇ dwɔŋ aṭal. Instead, there is a change of verb root.

(154)   S/A   VB

ḍeṇ   dwɔŋ   aṭa:t

female   big   PST^cook

The woman cooked.

In English, there is a similar situation syntactically. If we take transitive verbs such as 'eat', 'drink' or 'read', we can say:

(155)   I eat food   or   I eat

            I drink water   or   I drink

            I read a book   or   I read

The first clause is a transitive clause, the second, an uncomplemented form which Lyons (1971:252) describes as a PSEUDO-INTRANSITIVE. In this case, the object is not present, but may be contextually determined and may be recovered by semantic interpretation. This approach may be applied to Shilluk in a broader way. Instead of a handful of transitive verbs which have pseudo-intransitive counterparts, almost all transitive verbs in Shilluk have a pseudo-intransitive form.

It might be hypothesized that pseudo-intransitives were derived from transitive verbs. However, it will be shown that this will not work for Shilluk. In fact, the non-derivability of the Shilluk forms could be taken as evidence for claiming that pseudo-intransitives are never DERIVED structures in syntax. It will be shown later that the transitive and pseudo-intransitive (or FORM A and FORM B, as they will be termed later) are related, but synchronically underivable.

If we look more closely at the two possible verb forms in Shilluk, we see that in order to keep verb FORM A, there must be a complement. FORM B has no complement. For this reason, a complement (CMP) / non-complement (N-CMP) dichotomy seems appropriate.

It soon became clear, however, that this distinction was not the best. The FORM B verbs can, in fact, take two complements: the benefactive and the instrument as in (156).

Shilluk Phonology 75

(156) *ɲan ʈiṇ aʈalːa gincam* 'The girl cooked food.'
ɲan ʈiṇ ataːt 'The girl cooked.'
ɲan ʈiṇ atatːi meye 'The girl cooked for her mother.'
ɲan ʈiṇ ataːda dak 'The girl cooked with a pot.'

The verb 'to cook' [ʈal/ʈaːt] is used because the occurrence of suppletive forms makes the change more obvious. Other verbs which are not suppletive do change in similar fashion, but the change is less striking as in (157).

(157) *ya yepːa ɖɔ ɔt* 'I opened the door.'
ya yeːp 'I opened.'
ya yepːi meya 'I opened (it) for my mother.'
ya yeːba tɔŋ 'I opened (it) with a spear.'

Further examination reveals that the distinction is not one of the presence or absence of the CMP. Instead, it seems that perhaps optionality is the deciding factor and thus terms such as CMP-obligatory (C-OB) or CMP-optional (C-OPT) are preferable. In which case, the C-OB verb form would require a complement while a C-OPT verb form might or might not have a complement. However, further study has revealed that the distinction between forms is based on the presence or absence of the OBJECT rather than the complement. The C-OPT form cannot have a complement which is an object, but can have a benefactive or instrumental complement. However, we cannot term the forms WITH OBJECT or OBJECTLESS because of the VCMPCMP order. The verb form in the VCMPCMP order is the C-OPT form and there *is* an object in the second slot.

The only connection I have found so far between these two uses of the C-OPT form is that in both cases, the object can be said to have no close contact with the verb. Either the object is not present (SVCMP active order) or it is separated from the verb by an adposition (VCMPCMP). Thus, it is necessary to use some neutral terms such as FORM A and FORM B rather than C-OB and C-OPT.[12]

We began this section with the active SVCMP and based our analysis on that. If, however, we look at the passive form of the SVCMP, we find a second problem. The verb form of the passive is the same as the active. The complement/agent, however, is optional as in (158).

(158) *kwaṇ áʈal yi yan* 'The porridge was cooked by me.'
kwaṇ áʈal 'The porridge was cooked.'

---

[12]Any suggestions for what to call these verbs would be welcomed by the author.

In most cases, the agent is known from the context, and so the speaker does not bother to include this redundant information. The problem, then, is that in the case of the passive, the FORM A verb has an optional CMP component.

Fortunately, this situation is not totally unprecedented. Lyons (1971:378) states that all languages with passives have one thing in common—agentless sentences such as 'Bill was killed'. Since this phenomenon is not uncommon in the world's languages, FORM A can be redefined to allow for the passive construction to have an optional CMP/A.

The narrative word orders described above are a recent discovery, and it is not clear how all of the facts fit the FORM A/B system. The VCMPCMP takes FORM B; the active forms of the VSCMP take FORM A. It appears that the passive form also takes FORM A, but further investigation is needed to confirm this. Inclusion or exclusion of CMP's will have to be studied at a later time.

In (150), I began a diagram of the constituent orders of Shilluk verbs. Based on the discussion of complements, that diagram can now be completed (159).

(159)

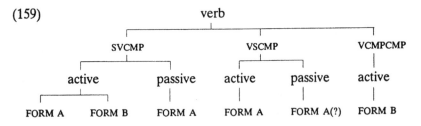

In both orders which have the s function, it is also possible to express both active and passive voice. The VCMPCMP order can only express the active voice.

Both voices in the VSCMP order *seem* to use FORM A of the verb. Further investigation needs to be done on this point as I am not completely sure which form is used in the passive.

In the SVCMP, the verb in the passive voice takes FORM A. In the active voice there is a choice. If there is a CMP slot, then FORM A is chosen; if no CMP slot, then FORM B is used. Other uses of FORM B have been noted. We have seen, then, that Shilluk has both sentences without subjects and sentences without complements.

Finally, the transitive and intransitive verbs can be identified structurally. The intransitive verbs have only one verb form which can be [±CMP]. Transitive verbs, on the other hand, have one form of the verb for [+CMP]

Shilluk Phonology 77

and another, underivable, but related form for [−CMP]. A diagram of this relationship is shown in (160).

(160)

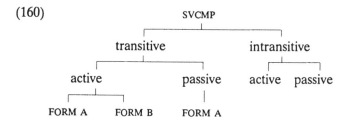

Word structure. Shilluk words may be from one to four syllables in length. Four-syllable words are usually compound words and they occur only rarely. It seems that the trend in Western Nilotic languages is to become monosyllabic wherever possible by incorporating affixes into the root (i.e., without loss of information). We will discuss roots in the next chapter. For now, we will concentrate on the affixes still remaining in the language.

Noun prefixes. The most common noun prefixes are a-, o-, ɲa- and ɲi-. These may at one time have been gender markers. They are frequently used in names to distinguish male and female and 'young' or 'child' as seen in the personal names in (161)–(162).

(161) MALE
ot̪ɔw
okoɲ[13]

(162) FEMALE
ɲat̪ɔw
ɲalam

(163) CATTLE
BULL	COW	CALF	COLOR/DESCRIPTION
obyẹc	abyẹc	ɲibyẹc	extra long horns
didu̱k	adu̱k	ɲidu̱k	dark gray

---

[13]Some words have not been marked for tone because it has not been possible to check the tone with native speakers.

It appears that the o- prefix is a masculine gender marker. The ɲi- or ɲa- is a feminine marker. The a- could also be assumed to be a feminine marker for animals. However, the system, if indeed there ever was one, is no longer productive as we see from (164)–(165).

(164) PERSONAL NAMES

	MALE	FEMALE	MALE OR FEMALE
	awụl	apar	aywɔk
	ajak	abụk	akwɔt
	awer	ayaṭ	amụm

(165) CATTLE NAMES

	BULL	COW	CALF	COLOR/DESCRIPTION
	ɲibɔŋ	obɔw	ɲibɔw	white one
	dila:l	ola:lɔ	ɲila:lɔ	red
	ditaŋ	ota:ŋɔ	ɲita:ŋɔ	black
	ocwɔt	cwɔt	ɲicwɔt	without horns

We see that now the a- prefix may occur before names of men or women. So, the assumption we had about a- turns out to be unfounded. The gender classification does not carry over into cow names since ɲi-, which is normally associated with calves or young bovines also identifies not the cow name, but the bull name. Even the o- has become associated with both male and female animals. Therefore, we conclude that the prefixes no longer have a productive role with regard to gender.

Prefixes appear to have been added to nouns simply as formatives to create other nouns as in (166).

(166)

gwɔ̂k	'dog'	ógwɔ̄k	'jackal'
bụl	'to mend'	àbụ̀l	'a patch'
lwē:dɔ̄	'finger'	álwē:dɔ̄	'crab'
àdè:rɔ̂	'donkey'	òdyèrɔ̂	'zebra'
ɲâŋ	'crocodile'	ɲáɲâŋ	'type of lizard'

There are also less common prefixes which perform this same function including ṭa-, ba-, and di-.

(167)

pīn	'wasp'	ṭápīn	'hornet'
jwan	'to hurry'	bājwân	'name meaning DO NOT HURRY'
cay	'to punish'	bàcáy	'name meaning NOT TO BE PUNISHED'
kɔmɔ	'behind'	dikɔmɔ	'back (part of body)'

Compound nouns. Compound words are often composed of a prefix and two nouns, or a prefix plus a verb and a noun. There are many possibilities, though only a couple of examples are given.

Shilluk Phonology   79

(168) *adẹ:ljwɔk* 'butterfly'

'Something/one that' seems to be the meaning of *a*-. The word *dẹ:l*
means 'skin' and *jwɔk* means 'God'; so a 'butterfly' has skin (that is so
delicate that it is) like God's skin.
    Another example is the word *aŋɔkrɔw* 'chameleon' which literally means
'something that vomits itself'.

Noun suffixes. In §3.1, we saw that -*ɔ* typically marks the singulative
while -*i* or a long root vowel marks the plural. There are also possessive
suffixes:

(169) SG   PL
       -*a*   -*wan* (inclusive)   '1st person'
                -*wɔn* (exclusive)
       -*i*   -*wųn*   '2nd person'
       -*e*   -*gen*   '3rd person'
       gɔn

When a possessed noun is singular, the tone on the possessive suffix is
M. If the possessed item is plural, then the possessive suffix has a H tone.
(170) is an example of the alternation of tone with the pronoun 'my'.

(170) *pà̠:mā*   'my sawn timber'
       pá̠m:á   'my sawn timbers'

There is also a referential determiner -*ání* 'this'. It is used as a marker
in discourse to identify the topic or major participant in a narrative. The
word *men* 'this' is used as the demonstrative.

Verb prefixes. Tense markers are prefixed to verb roots. The *á*- prefix
generally indicates the past tense and has a high tone.

(171) *ɲel ţiṇ áréŋā gàt*   'The boy ran to the river.'

The *o*- prefix usually indicates present or future tense. The tone of the
prefix is affected by constituent order so that the present tense *o*- has a M
tone in the active voice of the SVCMP order and a L tone in the passive
voice of the SVCMP order. There is a H tone in the future tense of the active
voice of the SVCMP.

80   Representation of Lexical Items

(172) SVCMP ACT   *jal dwɔŋ ōgwẹ̄:jɔ̄*   'The man clears (the field).'
      SV PASS   *pwɔ:ḍɔ ògwè:jɔ̀*   'The field is being cleared.'
      SV FORM B   *jal dwɔŋ ógwè̠:jị̀*   'The man will clear (the field).'

The prefix *ɲi-* is a habitual marker.

(173) *jaláni ɲicam:a rịŋɔ*   'This man always eats meat.'

In the event that both past tense and aspect occur together, the tense
marker precedes the aspect marker as *á-ɲi-* in the following sentence.

(174) *gik áɲigɔk:i yị en*   'Things were habitually done by him.'

Verb suffixes. There are three suffixes which may occur with verbs. The
-*a* suffix follows the verb in SVCMP active.

(175) *ḍeṇ dwɔŋ áṭal:a rịŋɔ*   'The woman cooked the meat.'

An -*ɔ* suffix often occurs with FORM B. There is also an -*i* suffix which
occurs with these and other verbs. The functions of these suffixes are
unclear at this time.

Kohnen's explanation of the -*i* emphasizes that there is a difference
between the shortened *yi* → *i* meaning 'by' which follows the verb and the
suffix -*i*. He lists three possible uses of the -*i* suffix: 1) direct object
pronominal suffix, 2) final vowel of the past tense of some intransitive
verbs, 3) the subject (personal pronouns, suffix 2s) in subjunctive sentences
when the subject follows the verb (1933:137).

The -*ɔ* suffix, according to Kohnen (1933:124), is added to all qualitative
(FORM B) verbs in the present and futures tenses, but is dropped in the past
tense. The -*ɔ* also is added to the applicative (FORM A) to make a passive
in the present tense, but is dropped in the future and past tenses. From
(177), it can be seen that both suffixes are used, and no difference in
meaning is readily apparent. More work needs to be done in this area. The
-*i* does appear consistently with the benefactive verb form which is derived
from FORM B. Suffixes -*ɔ* and -*i* are seen in (176) and (177).

(176) *jal dwɔŋ ōgwẹ̄:jɔ̄*   'The man clears (the field).'
      ya tāṭ:ị́ mea   'I cook for my mother.'

(177) *jaláni ōcwɔ̀t:ị*   'The man calls.'
      jaláni ōcwɔ̀t:ɔ̀   'The man calls.'

Shilluk Phonology

3.2 Lexical items

In this section we will be considering the morphophonology of the nominal system of Shilluk as well as that of the verbal system, though to a lesser extent. The various grammars written about Shilluk have tried to explain the system of singulars and plurals though the discussion rapidly deteriorates to a listing of the IRREGULARITIES of the system. The end result for the language learner is virtual chaos. It would seem that this problem extends across most Nilotic languages as can be seen from these instructions for learning nouns in the nominal system of Dholuo:

> Although certain rules do exist, governing the formation of the plural of nouns, there are also numerous irregularities. Because of this difficulty, the student will do well, if when learning the singular form of the noun, he also memorizes the plural form 1. This will prove extremely helpful in the beginning, whilst one is gradually becoming acquainted with the rules governing the regular nouns (Anonymous 1935).

A similar word of caution is brought by Fr. Kohnen in his Shilluk grammar when he says "A general rule for the formation of plurals in Shilluk cannot be given. Practically one has to learn the plural of nouns from the dictionary...below (are) some practical guidelines" (Kohnen, 1933:19). He then goes on to list about fifteen ways to form a plural in Shilluk.

The conclusions reached in this chapter, in a sense, only confirm what Kohnen and others have said. In fact, it will go much further and claim that each noun has two UNDERLYING REPRESENTATIONS, one for singular and another for plural. Neither form can be successfully derived from the other. Extensive evidence will be given to support this claim, with further evidence offered in chapter 4. While most of this section will deal with nouns, we will also consider the A and B forms of the verb. We will see that the same principles apply to both nouns and verbs. Thus, our conclusions apply to both the nominal and verbal systems.

Points of consistency. We begin our study by looking for points of similarity between forms. The first point, word shape, deals primarily with nouns. Verbs have aspect and tense prefixes, and clearly these do not function in the same way as nominal prefixes. Any verb may have tense/aspect markers, but the lexical meaning of the verb itself is unchanged. However, the addition of a prefix to a noun root may change the semantic meaning.

82   Representation of Lexical Items

Word shape. In §3.1, we saw how the addition of a nominal prefix changed the meaning of the word. The word shape, with regard to the prefix and the root of a particular word, remains consistent in both the singular and plural forms as seen in (178).

(178) SG   PL

gwɔ̂k	*gwɔ̂:k*	'dog/s'
ógwɔ̄k	*ógɔ̂:kì*	'jackal/s'
lwē:dɔ̄	*lwêt*	'finger/s'
álwē:dɔ̄	*álwêt*	'crab/s'

If there is a prefix in the singular, there is also one in the plural. When speaking of word shape, I am referring *only* to the presence or absence of a prefix to the root. The end of the word is less consistent in shape.

Initial root consonant. The second point of consistency has to do with the root itself. The root of a Shilluk word has a shape c_1vc_2. The c_1 may be a sequence of a consonant + glide or simply a single c. In most instances, the singular and plural forms will have the same c_1 as in (179).

(179) SG   PL

bêlɔ̄	*bēl*	'taste/s'
byè:rɔ̄	*byēr*	'root/s'
gûr	*gṳ̀:r*	'Nile perch/es'
gyè̱k	*gyè̱:k*	'Nile lechwe/s'

The same generalization holds in the verb root between the FORM A and FORM B.

(180) FORM A   FORM B

kak	*ka̱:k*	'split'
kwa:n	*kwa̱:n*	'count'
cak	*ca̱k:i̱*	'start'
cwak	*cwa̱k:i̱*	'support'
cya̱k	*cya̱k:i̱*	'name'

The reader may have noticed a slight change in the tenor of the language used between the first and second points just discussed. The first point is consistent in all cases, except, of course, suppletive forms. The second point, having to do with the c_1, is consistent *in most instances.* In other words, there are exceptions. In the next two points, this same assumption is necessary. The points of similarity are the general rule.

Shilluk Phonology

83

However, there are fairly frequent exceptions to them which will be discussed in the section on differences.

Final root consonant. The c_2 of the root is generally the same phoneme in both forms of the word. Look again at (179) and (180). The c_2 may be doubled, or geminate intervocalically as in *cak*, *cwak*, and *cyak*. However, the segment is the same in both forms. There is a difference in voicing with the plosives, but they can be shown to be the same underlying segment. The various rules dealing with voicing in plosives were covered in chapter 2.

Root vowel. In order to discuss the root vowel, a convention needs to be proposed. In most cases, [EX] does not correlate with changes in vowel height. The only exception to that is the [o] which is [−EX] and the [u̱] which is [+EX]. For the purposes of this discussion, I will identify [o] as a [+HI, −EX] vowel and the [u̱] as [+HI, +EX]. This convention will allow us to discuss VOWEL HEIGHT without having to constantly account for the vowel height which is directly related to the [EX] feature.

Let us look now at the vowel height as it occurs in the root (i.e., I E A Ɔ O).[14] We find that the vowel height is usually the same in both forms.

(181)		SG	PL	
	/I/	*cìŋɔ̀*	*cíŋ*	'hand/s'
	/E/	*àdè:rɔ̀*	*àdè:r*	'donkey/s'
	/A/	*bâ̱ŋ*	*bâ̱:ŋ*	'servant/s'
	/Ɔ/	*ápwɔ̀:jɔ̀*	*ápwɔ̂c:i̱*	'rabbit/s'
	/O/	*gûr*	*gu̱:r*	'Nile perch/es'

(182)		FORM A	FORM B	
	/I/	*li̱t*	*li̱t:i*	'see'
	/E/	*gwẹc*	*gwẹ:c*	'clear a field'
	/A/	*bak*	*ba:k*	'guess'
	/Ɔ/	*cɔŋ*	*cɔ̱:ŋ*	'dance'
	/O/	*cok*	*cok*	'stop on the way'

We see that vowel height is the same in both forms. It does not take long, however, to see that there are differences in length and in the feature [EXPANDED]. We will look at these as we discuss the differences between forms.

---

[14]Here, and throughout the paper, upper case letters will be used to identify segments which are not fully specified for a feature, such as [EX] in the case of vowels.

84   Representation of Lexical Items

Points of variability. We have seen that there are a number of similarities between singular and plural forms and also between FORM A and FORM B verbs. Now, we will examine how these forms differ. As with most natural languages, there are suppletive forms, or words in which it is not possible to show a relationship between morphemes by means of a general rule. The forms involved have different roots (Crystal 1985). Shilluk has such words as seen in (183).

(183) SG   PL
       gìn   jā̰m:ḭ̄   'thing/s'
       gɔ́l   kā̰l:ḭ̄   'household/s'

These words are obviously suppletive, i.e., derived from different roots. When positing different underlying representations for words in Shilluk, I am not suggesting that all forms are suppletive but that there is no way to write a general rule to derive the forms in the way that is commonly expected. The following sections will show the distinctions that must be listed in the lexicon while maintaining the claim that the words are intrinsically related, i.e., historically cognate.

Initial root consonant. We have said that the c_i may be a single consonant or a sequence of consonant + glide. In most words, the choice is one or the other for both forms. However, with some words, there is a change which is not predictable. One form will have a c + glide; the other form will have only a c. There seems to be no general way to account for the missing glide. Consider (184) and (185).

(184) SG   PL
       cwôr   cɔ̀:r   'blind person/people'
       cwɔ̂t   cɔ̀:t   'cow/s without horns'
       pyḛ̄n   pén:ḭ̄   'sleeping skin/s'
       pyèr   pêr:ḭ   'lower back/s'

(185) FORM A   FORM B
       koɲ   kwṵɲḭ   'help'
       gwɔk   go:k   'work'

In previous examples, we have seen that in general, the onset is the same in either form of a word. In (184) and (185), however, there is an exception to the rule. Within the set of nouns which displays onset alternation, the singular form has the c + glide while the plural words have a simple onset. In verbs, there is no particular lexical pattern.

Shilluk Phonology 85

There are two ways to account for this alternation. First, it is possible to set up two underlying representations for these forms. The appropriate form is learned for each and no attempt is made to derive one from the other. The second option is to set up a zero alternation rule which could account for the data.

Probably the most common way to handle a zero alternation is to simply delink the segment when it should not surface. However, in order to write a rule for such a delinking, one would need a conditioning environment. The Shilluk data do not suggest such an environment, and so it would be necessary to indicate lexically which words, and which form of those lexical items would undergo this delinking rule. Thus, the conditioning variable for consonant delinking could not be phonological in the case of Shilluk.

Another possibility is to handle the zero alternation in Shilluk as a morphologically based rule. It would mean that FORM A of a word would have the segment delinked while FORM B kept the segment attached to the timing tier. The data in (184) suggest that the plural form delinks the glide while the singular does not delink it. Even in these examples, however, it would be necessary to indicate these words in the lexicon because not all singular/plural pairs with glides would undergo this rule.

Additionally, the TRANSITIVE verbs would present a serious problem because the glide delinking could apply to either form depending on the lexical item (185).

We will see from other data that independent underlying representation are necessary for singulars and plurals as well as for verb forms. Because this is the case, incorporating this information into the underlying representation does not actually complicate the analysis further.

Final root consonant. While most words have an invariant c_2 in the root between forms, there are some exceptions to this principle. The most common type of variation is an alternation between [l] and [t] and between [r] and [t]. Below are examples of non-alternating c_2 forms, (186), followed by the alternating ones, (187). This alternation was referred to in §2.2 when discussing the distinctive features necessary for Shilluk.

(186) SG   PL

gɔ̄:l	gɔ̄:l	'wild dog/s'
acwi̱l	acwi̱:l	'brown cow/s'
bāt	ba̱:t	'arm/s'
gwar	gwa:r	'to snatch' (FORM A/B)
ḍur	ḍur	'to push'

86   Representation of Lexical Items

(187)   SG   PL

SG	PL	
lwɔ́l	lɔ́t	'gourd/s'
pāl	pât	'spoon/s'
kâːl	kâ̱ːt	'cattle camp/s'
maːr	ma̱ːt	'to love' (FORM A/B)
gwiːr	gwi̱ːt	'to prepare'
cwɔl	cwɔṯːi̱	'to call'
tyel	tye̱ṯːi̱	'to pull'

In (186), we see that c_2 is the same in both words. However, in (187) there is an alternation in c_2 from [l] or [r] to [t] and are accounted for by a rule discussed in chapter 5. It will be shown that these alternating final consonants must be indicated in the underlying representation. The segment will be marked as an archisegment (i.e., an underspecified segment). As a matter of convenience, these archisegments will be transcribed with upper case letters such as /L/ and /R/.

There are a few other words which show an alternation in the c_2 though the pattern is somewhat erratic. It is assumed that the c_2 of these words would have to be included in the underlying representation and could not be predicted by rule. Some of these words are listed in (188).

(188)   SG   PL

SG	PL	
dyèl	dyê̱k	'goat/s'
lèːjɔ̀	lēk	'tooth/teeth'
dway	dwat	'moon/months'
wīc	wâ̱ṯ	'heads'
yoː	ye̱ːṯ	'road/s'
mey	me̱ːk	'mother/s'
wiy	weːk	'father/s'

Root vowel. Now we turn from consonants to the root vowel. First, we will look at the feature [expanded]. Then, we will examine the changes in the vowel itself.

If we wished to derive plurals from singulars or vice versa, we would need to be able to predict the [±EX] value of the root vowels. The reader will recall that there are two sets of five vowels, repeated here for convenience.

(189)   [−EX]   [+EX]

        i   o   i̱   u̱

        e   ɔ   e̱   ɔ̱

            a   a̱

Shilluk Phonology   87

In order to derive singular/plural nouns or FORM A/B verbs, we must either
have the same [EX] feature on the vowel or be able to give a rule for any
change of that feature. Let us look at the data.

(190) SG   PL   [EX]
       ókwɔ̄r   ókɔ̂r:ì   'serval'   (−) (−)
       ákɔ̀ɲ   ákɔ̄ɲ:ì   'gazelle'
       kél   kè:l   'cheetah'
       mɔ̀k   mɔ̂:k   'type of fish'

(191) ɲâŋ   ɲáŋ:ī̠   'crocodile'   (−) (+)
       káŋ   kâŋ:ì̠   'trumpet'
       gwɔ̄k   gwɔ̠̂:k   'work'
       bák   bà̠:k   'garden'

(192) ŋṳ̀:   ŋúr:ī̠   'lion'   (+) (+)
       pà̠m   pám:ī̠   'table'
       yḛ́p   yḛ̂:p   'tail'
       gwɔ̠̂k   gwɔ̠̂:k   'dog'

(193) pyḛ̄n   pén:ī̠   'sleeping skin'   (+) (−)
       ṭwɔ̠̄l   ṭól:ī̠   'snake'

From these examples, we see that in (190) both singular and plural are
[−EX] values. In (191), however, the singular is [−EX] while the plural is
[+EX]. In (192), both sets are the same, though this time both are [+EX].
In (193), the singular is [+EX] while the plural is [−EX]. This last set is
the rarest, but it does occur. In short, [aEX] → [aEX] and [aEX] → [−aEX].
The feature [EX] is not predictable, and both values must be represented
in the lexical entries.

We have described the situation for nouns, but what about verbs? Can
we predict the [EX] value in FORM A and FORM B verbs? Consider the data.

(194) FORM A   FORM B   [EX]
       ban   ba:n   'roll'   (−) (−)
       gɔc   gɔc:i   'hit'
       liṭ   liṭ:i   'see'

(195) yep   ye̠:p   'open'   (−) (+)
       kor   ku̠r   'watch'
       gam   ga̠m:i̠   'catch'
       gɔɲ   gɔ̠:ɲ   'untie'

(196)	gac	ga:c	'mark'	(+) (+)
	bɔy	bɔy:i	'try'	
	rap	ra:p	'burn'	

| (197) | cwɔp | cop:i | 'stab once' | (+) (−) |

Again, we see that all four possibilities are available. The (+ −) combination is very rare, and seems to also correlate with alternations in the c_1 position. There is also a VOWEL HEIGHT change.

Out of 66 nouns chosen at random, 25 were (− −) [EX], 27 were (+ +), 12 were (− +) and 2 were (+ −). Of 55 verbs, 7 were (− −), 19 were (+ +), 28 were (− +) and 1 was (+ −). According to these figures, 79% of nouns are predictable but only 47% of verbs. These figures suggest an appreciable margin for error for the language learner were he or she to assume predictability. It would seem the wisest course of action to assign the [EX] feature as a vowel feature in the underlying representation for both forms of nouns and verbs.

There are occasions when not only is the [EX] feature not predictable, but even the vowel height changes. Consider the words in (198).

(198)	SG	PL	
	beṭ	biṭ:i	'fish spear/s'
	bò:ḍɔ̀	bɔ̂:ṭì	'craftsman/men'
	cɔ̀:gɔ́	cūw	'bone/s'
	óbwɔ̂rɔ̀	óbwūr	'type of grass'
	òkɔ̀ḍɔ̀	ókūṭ:ì	'hedgehog/s'
	rè:jɔ́	ríc	'fish'
	ṭwɔ̄l	ṭól:ī	'snake/s'
	áṭíwī	àṭèw	'small container/s'
	kwéy	kwà:y	'grandfather/s'
	cṹŋ	cɔ̂ŋ	'knee/s'

(199)	FORM A	FORM B	
	kɔɲ	kwuɲ:i	'help'
	jɔli	juṭ:i	'repeat'
	cwɔp	cop:i	'stab once'
	bel	bit:i	'taste'
	rep	rip	'add'
	dɔm	dum	'save'

In these words there are alternations between the following vowels:

Shilluk Phonology

(200) e ~ i   e ~ a   ɔ ~ u̞
     e ~ i̞   o ~ ɔ̞   ɔ ~ o
     e̞ ~ i   u̞ ~ ɔ   ɔ̞ ~ u̞
     i̞ ~ e   ɔ̞ ~ o

or factoring out [EX],

(201) E ~ I
      O ~ ɔ
      E ~ A

There does not seem to be any pattern of correlation between the [EX] value and this alternation in vowel height since both [EX] values seem to be equally involved. The vowels are not exclusively high or low, front or back. The majority of alternations involve front vowels with front vowels (I~E) and back vowels with back vowels (O~ɔ) or unrounded vowels with unrounded vowels (E~A). Since there is no predictable pattern or even a restriction on variability that could easily be placed on these words, we must again opt for representing both forms in the underlying representation.

It would appear that, in a McCarthian model, Shilluk vowels could be said to have morphemic status since they are highly independent and lexically significant. Elements encoded into the vowel morpheme are the [EX] and vowel height features.

Tone. The last point to consider is tone. Tone is a feature assigned to the root; thus, it is considered separately from the root vowel. The tone is eventually realized on the vowel which is the tone bearing unit. In order to assure that tone is associated in the correct x slot, (202) spells out the tone association among the syllable head, x slot, vowel and tone.

(202)

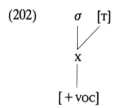

This representation states that tone can only be linked to an x slot which is also associated with *both* a syllable head and a segment with [+VOC] content. If either of these elements is absent, then the tone cannot be linked to that x slot.

90　　　　　　　　　　　　　　　　　　　Representation of Lexical Items

Since there is a grammatically significant role of tone in the verbs, we will only consider tone on the nouns. It would be helpful to the language learner if tone were predictable between singular and plural forms. However, it seems that Shilluks are able to cope with a considerable amount of unpredictable behavior with regard to the tone. It is a rare experience to find a singular/plural pair which has the same tone.

We will begin our discussion with words with at least one H tone in the singular.

(203)

TONE	SG	PL	
H-H	kwér	kwé:r	'small lizard/s'
ĤL-ĤL	gwɔ̰̂k	gwɔ̰̂:k	'dog/s'
HL-ĤL	gḛ́:lɔ̰̀	gḛ̂:l	'riverbank/s'
HM-HM	ápɔ̰́:dḭ̄	ápôt:ḭ̄	'calabash/es'

(204)

H-L	kél	kè:l	'cheetah/s'
H-M̂L	bák	bâ̰:k	'garden/s'
H-LL̂H	dítáŋ	dìtă̰:ŋ	'black bull/s'
HL-M̂L	cṵ́rɔ̰̀	cṵ̀r	'eel-like catfish/es'
HM-ĤL	bā̰:ɲɔ̰̄	bâ̰:ɲ	'grasshopper/s'

In (203), we see that H, ĤL and HM have identical tone patterns in singular and plural. However, in (204), we see quite a different story. The H in the singular may correspond to L, M̂L, L̂H in the plural while ĤL has a plural counterpart of M̂L. Further, a singular HM may have a plural with ĤL. This is not a complete listing of the possibilities, but the sample here is representative of the problem. As such, we could end the argument here. But it is useful to see the extent of the problem.

Moving on to the M tone, we find a similar situation to that of the H tone.

(205)

TONE	SG	PL	
M-HM	kyēɲ	kyéɲ:ḭ̄	'horse/s'
M-M̂L	jwɔ̄k	jwɔ̰̀:k	'god/s'
M̂L-H	ḓɔ̰̀ŋɔ̰̀	ḓɔ̰́ŋ	'basket/s'
M̂H-M̂L	gɔ̰̄:l	gɔ̰̀:l	'wild dog/s'
	bā̰t	bà̰:t	'arm/s'

(206)　M̂L-ML　　bà̰:r　　bār:ì　　'tall' (SG/PL)

There are no cases with a level M in both singular and plural words. There are identical ML sets (206). More commonly, however, we see that

Shilluk Phonology

91

M in the singular can be matched with HM, M̂L or H in the plural. Again, not all options are listed.

Now consider singulars with L tone. The tones may be the same as in (207). However, in most cases, the tones will be distinctly different. In (208), note that a singular L may correspond to M, H, L̂H, and M̂L in the plural. Likewise, in (209) LH may go with H, M, or HL̂.

(207)	TONE	SG	PL	
	L-L	*gyè̠k*	*gyè̠:k*	'Nile lechwe/s'
	L-L	*gɔ̀k*	*gɔ̀:k*	'white skin bracelet/s'
(208)	L-M	*ḓɔ̀ŋɔ̀*	*ḓɔ̄ŋ*	'Juba person/people'
	L-H	*cìŋɔ̀*	*cíŋ*	'hand/s'
	L-L̂H	*kṳ̀l*	*kṳ̌l*	'pig/s'
	L-M̂L	*lò̠:ṭ*	*lɔ̠̄ṭ*	'club/s'
(209)	LH-H	*byè̠:lɔ̌*	*byél*	'millet'
	LH-M	*cɔ̀:gɔ̌*	*cṳ̄w*	'bone/s'
	L̂H-HL̂	*kǐy*	*kîy*	'plant/s with edible roots'

If we consider only surface level tones for the moment, we find that we have the following correspondences between singular and plural.

(210)			Plural tone		
			H	M	L
Singular		H	X		X
tone		M	sequences only		
		L	X	X	X

We see that H singular tones may be H or L in the plural. L singular tones may be H, M or L in the plural. That much seems highly irregular. But then, M singular tone cannot have M plural tone! That in itself would push us toward the position that the underlying tone must be represented independently in the lexicon. There seems to be no way to predict it. Given this high degree of independence and the fact that certain tones correlate with grammatical features, tone would seem to have morphemic status. Therefore, we must have the morpheme for tone, and the vocalic morpheme including the vowel height and the [EX] feature listed for *both* singular and plural forms.

3.3 Underlying representation

Having looked at the data, it is now time to try to formulate the lexical entries for nouns and verbs. Shilluk is a language with extreme tendencies to multiple variation. In the previous sections, it has become clear that consonants, vowels, and tone vary within lexical items. In some cases, the variation is also grammatical since certain tones and initial consonants may each distinguish number.

McCarthy (1982:192ff) argues that morphemes should be represented on separate tiers. Further, he suggests that even the canonical pattern or prosodic template of the lexical item can be considered a tier in its own right. Evidence presented in chapter 4 will show that this same argument is relevant to the Shilluk data. For the moment, however, it seems advantageous to represent tone, consonants, and vowels on separate tiers. Each of these tiers represents a lexical variable and thus, combined, these tiers are all required to identify a lexically significant morpheme.

(211)

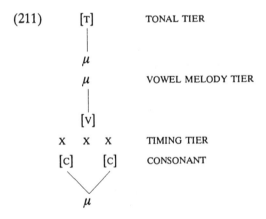

Within this representation, it will be necessary to include information regarding the x slot with the syllable head. It is assumed in this study that the syllable head is present in the underlying representation. The vowel features would associate to the syllable head.

One notational problem needs to be dealt with here. Generally, the notation used to indicate a syllable head is a perpendicular line over the appropriate x slot. However, given the two-dimensional restrictions of the paper on which it is drawn, the (ẋ) configuration could easily be assumed to be an association line. Therefore, I propose to underscore the x̱ slot to indicate that there is a syllable head associated with it.

Shilluk Phonology 93

The [EX] feature is a subvariant feature which attaches to the vowel and does not appear to have morphemic status. Therefore, the [EX] feature will be shown in the representation as being associated to the vocalic tier. Below is the representation including the [EX] feature and the new notation for the syllable head.

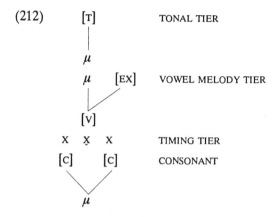

Finally, we have seen evidence that affixes are also morphemes in Shilluk. Again, these morphemes may be on separate tiers. However, these additional tiers will seriously complicate the task of representing it on paper. Therefore, when affixes are added, they will be marked with a (μ) and tagged.

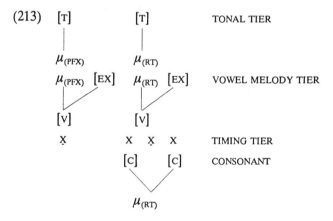

The root itself, as it refers to the CVC pattern, is made up of several morphemes; namely, the vowel, consonants, and tone. This set of morphemes can be taken together to make up a root. This root can then be combined with other sets of morphemes to form other structures. For example, the root and the number (NM) suffix combine to form a stem. This stem will be represented by a THETA (θ). The addition of a prefix requires yet another level; namely, the word (ω). Already the representation is becoming difficult to manage so I will show this aspect of it separately.

(214)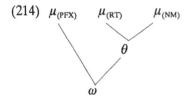

We will see in chapter 5 that there is a special phonological significance to the 'stem' and therefore, it must be indicated.

One further complication in the representation is that most of the words in Shilluk will require dual representation for singular and plural and for FORM A and FORM B verbs. The representations will be side by side. For the sake of consistency, the singular will be on the left and the plural to the right for nouns. FORM A will be on the left and FORM B on the right for verbs.

We are assuming that there are no bundles of features. Each feature may have its own plane or tier. However, it will be necessary to consider several features together in the identification of a particular phoneme. Where it is relevant, the features will be listed. However, for the convenience of the reader, letter symbols will also be used as an abbreviation for the feature complexes.

We will now work through the various parts of the representation step by step, beginning with the consonant melody tier.

In most cases, the c_1 and c_2 are identical in both forms of singular and plural. The representation reflects that similarity for [gwɔ̂k] [gwɔ̂:k] 'dog/s'.

(215)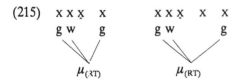

As discussed earlier, however, sometimes the onsets are not the same. In these cases, the representations will be distinctly different, as in the case of [pyęn] [pen:i] 'sleeping skin/s'.

Shilluk Phonology

(216)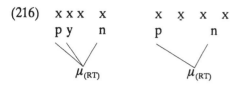

Then, we need to fill in the root vowel. First, we will indicate the symbol representing the underlying vowel height (using upper case letters). The feature [EX] will be attached to the segment. Tone is on a separate tier, but will be indicated above the timing tier and above the vowel tier since it will eventually be realized on the vowel. We continue with the same words as above.

(217a)   (217b)

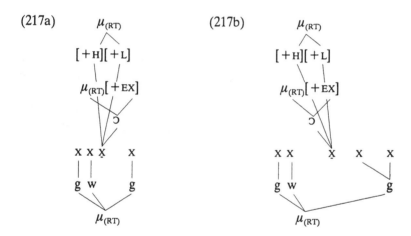

96 Representation of Lexical Items

(218a) (218b)

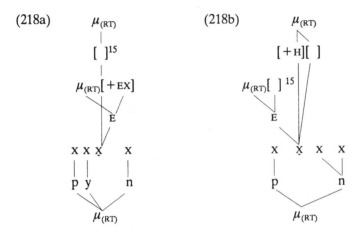

Since nominal prefixes are no longer part of a productive word formation process, we will need to incorporate the prefix into our word in the lexicon. We will keep the prefix distinct from the stem by means of (PFX) tag on the morphemes associated with it. For the moment, the tone and [EX] feature will be assigned to the prefix. There is a discussion of this process in chapter 5. The underlying representation for [álwē:dɔ́] [álwêt] 'crab/s' is shown in (219).

---

[15]The underspecified tone will be filled in by complement rules and will be realized as [−HI,−LO]. Likewise, the underspecified [EX] value will be filled in as [−EX].

Shilluk Phonology

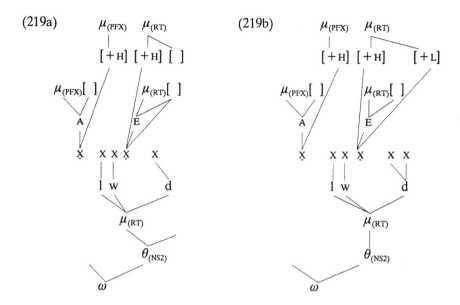

In §3.1., it was explained that there are three sets of nouns. Words need to be marked in the lexicon so that the appropriate suffixes can be added. Therefore, each noun root must have a marking for noun set 1, 2, or 3.

In (219), noun set 2 (NS2) is indicated. Set 2 has singulative and neutral forms. Therefore, the singulative would receive the -ɔ suffix by rule. A set 1 word would receive the -i suffix on the plural. Set 3 words would receive both singulative and plural suffixes. It may be necessary to add a fourth set for words which have no number suffix in either singular or plural form.

In all cases, the plural would have a geminate c_2 in the root. It may not be retained throughout the derivation, but it will always be in the underlying representation as a marker for plurality.

There is only one remaining point which has not been touched on. This point involves the length of the root vowel. It will be noticed in the previous example that the root vowels are of different lengths. This difference can be explained by means of syllable structure. Syllable structure is a complex issue in itself and is covered in chapter 4. We will find that syllable structure must also be marked in the lexicon. In most cases, the same syllable structure will apply to both forms. But, as seems to be the rule for Shilluk, there will also be a few exceptions to that.

4

Shilluk Syllable Structure

In the preceding chapter, we saw that there are some variations in the length of the root vowel. In order to account for these and other changes in derived forms, we must examine the role of syllable structure in Shilluk. We will see that the syllable structure has a pervasive influence throughout the phonology. Indeed, syllable structure is probably the most important aspect of Shilluk phonology. Let us begin examining this key to Shilluk by looking at the surface possibilities.

4.1. Surface overview

At first glance, the syllable shapes in Shilluk do not appear to be problematic. The most common syllable pattern is cvc. Below are listed words which represent the surface representations of the various patterns.

(220)			v			$ \underline{u} $	'and'
		c	v			$ y\underline{i} $	'you (SG)'
			v	c		ɔt	'house'
		c	v	c		beṭ	'fish spear'
		c	v	v	c	bu̱:r	'grave, hole'
	c	c	v	v	c	kwe:r	'small hoe'

Such a listing of surface patterns does not provide us with a formal apparatus for adequately discussing the subject of syllable structure. Instead, recognition of a separate tier dealing with syllable structure seems to be the most enlightening way to approach the matter.

99

4.2. Syllable structure tier

As with other tiers, the syllable structure tier is associated with the timing tier. It is a basic assumption that in the underlying representation, words are only partially syllabified. It will be assumed that x slots in the underlying representation are preassociated with the syllable heads. In order to simplify the representations, c and v tiers will be shown together. Also, since syllable structure is being emphasized in this chapter, other tiers will be conflated to conserve space and to improve clarity. Thus, we might begin with an underlying representation as in (221).

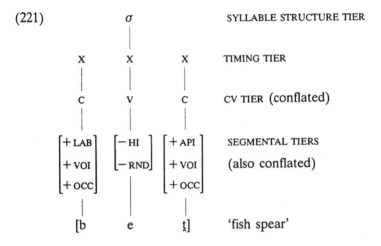

Notice that the syllable head is attached to a row of x's. These x's represent timing slots. The timing slots are then associated with a CV TIER. We see that having the syllable structure in place effectively eliminates the need to have the CV TIER as the syllable structure will define the vowels. When the syllable structure is fully in place, the consonants and vowels will be defined by that structure. Thus, in the future, the c and v tiers will not be given. Next, we see that feature complexes are associated with the timing tier. In the interest of conserving space, the phonological symbols (§3.3) will be used on this level to represent these feature complexes whenever the features in question are not particularly relevant to the discussion.

The syllable (σ) is made up of the onset (o) and the rime (R). The onset is anything to the left of the syllable head. The rime is composed of the syllable head, sometimes termed the nucleus, plus anything to the right of the syllable head. Following Noske (1982), I will assume that the onset-rime distinction is

Shilluk Phonology   101

a universal of syllable structure. The process for syllabification, then, will have two parts.

"a. Co-syllabify all x's to the left of the syllable head subject to the language-specific constraints governing onsets.

b. Co-syllabify all x's to the right of the syllable head subject to the language-specific constraints governing rhyme structure." (Hayward 1986:312).

Continuing with the example above, the first step is to co-syllabify the onset.

(222)

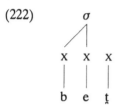

The last step, then is to co-syllabify the rime.

(223)

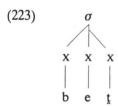

For the purposes of this study, a syllable will consist of an onset (o) and rime (R). The rime is composed of a nucleus (N) and a coda (co). Syllable heads will usually be shown with a vertical line (|). (The only exceptions to the notation convention described here are to be found in chapter 3 and in chapter 5). Any line shown at an angle is intended to indicate either onset (/) or coda (\) in its relation to the nucleus.

(224)

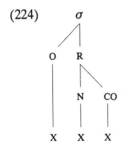

It was decided in chapter 2 that the onset consonant plus glide was a sequence rather than a single unit. In the schematic representation, I will use two x slots in the onset which may be filled by a sequence of a consonant and a glide ([w] or [y]). The representation is shown in (225a). Had I chosen to interpret the c + glide as a unit, only one x slot would have been needed. The representation for that unit is shown in (225b).

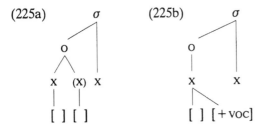

We may assume that it is always possible to have a sequence of consonants in the onset. In order to simplify the representation, examples without the sequence will be shown with only one x since the glide is optional. Where it is relevant, both x slots will be included in rules.

4.3. Syllable template

It has been assumed that the syllable is only partly specified in the underlying representation. Particularly, only the syllable head is supplied. From this point, we need some further guidelines for implementing the syllabification process with regard to language-specific constraints. One way to do this is to specify a maximal syllable template for the language such as the template in (226).

Shilluk Phonology

(226)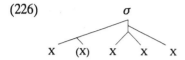

The structure in (226) would account for the maximally possible syllable in Shilluk (e.g., *kweːr* 'small hoe'). We might generalize this template to account for all other possible syllable patterns by indicating certain x slots as optional. We would then have an overall Shilluk syllable template like the one shown below.

(227)

Having developed this general structural template, we find that it is not terribly revealing. The only definitive bits of information which we can gather are that (1) codas do not branch, and (2) every syllable has a nucleus, and that is not unexpected. Therefore, let us examine the problem from a less generalized perspective.

In fact, Shilluk requires two distinct syllable templates, a crucial element of the more marked of which must be indicated in the underlying representation. The two templates are shown below.

(228a)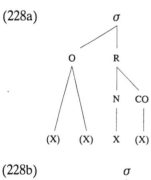

(228b)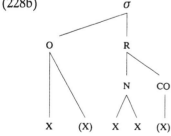

104   Shilluk Syllable Structure

(228a) will account for cv, v, vc, cvc and cvv patterns. (228b) accounts
for cvv and cvvc. There is an overlap with respect to cvv, but it will
become clear later why there are two cvv patterns (see §4.5.).

As mentioned earlier, one of these templates is more marked than the
other. But how can such templates be evaluated in terms of markedness?
Kaye and Lowenstamm (1981) and Noske (1982:271) have discussed
theories of syllable markedness. Noske's hierarchy is given in (229).

(229)   ONSET   RIME   MARKEDNESS VALUE
          C   V   0
          Ø   V C   1
         C C   V C C   2
        C C C   V C C C   3
       $C_1 \ldots C_n$ $VC_1 \ldots C_n$ n

The thrust of the arguments of all these investigators is that requiring
the syllabification algorithm to define syllables having the lowest possible
markedness value provides a constraint for making empirical predictions
that can be tested for the phonologies of natural languages. Kaye and
Lowenstamm as well as Noske say that vc and vv would be equally
complex. Likewise, vcc and vvc would be equal as well.

This theory, then, would account for the fact that the second template
cvvc is more rare since it contains more timing slots and thus more weight
in the rime. We could eliminate the second template except for the overlap
of vv in both. The syllabification of vv in (228a) is more common than that
of vv in (228b). Further discussion on this point may be found in §4.5.

4.4. Restrictions and constraints

We will find that many of the phonological rules in Shilluk are controlled
by the syllable structure. It is vital to the discussion in the remainder of
this chapter to establish the restrictions and constraints which apply to
Shilluk. We will review the restrictions and constraints for the onset and
then discuss the constraints for the syllable head and coda.

Onset constraints. The constraints placed on the onset position were
covered in chapter 2. They are repeated here for the reader's convenience.
The first constraint concerns the sequences of consonants which are allowed in the onset slot.

Shilluk Phonology

(230) INITIAL CONSONANT SEQUENCE

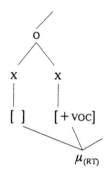

Two constraints are placed on the initial root sequences.

(231) INITIAL CONSONANT SEQUENCE CONSTRAINT

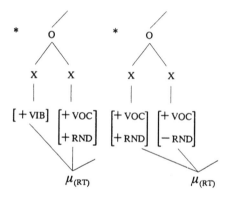

(230) allows for any consonant to be followed by a glide [+voc]. The more specific constraints would then apply such that *[rw] and *[wy] would not be allowed. Further, a geminate consonant cannot occur initially in a root.

(232) INITIAL GEMINATE CONSONANT CONSTRAINT

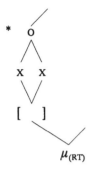

Finally, we have a constraint which involves the onset and the nucleus. Since this constraint involves the onset, it will be included in this section. It is stated as follows.

(233) GLIDE AND VOWEL CONSTRAINT

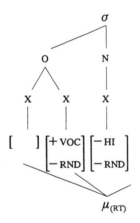

In this constraint, the [y] glide may only be followed by [−HI, −RND] vowels.

Syllable head constraint. If two timing units are associated with one syllable head, they must have the same feature matrix. This fact remains in force regardless of whether template (228a) or (228b) is under consideration.

Shilluk Phonology

(234) SYLLABLE HEAD CONSTRAINT (SHC)

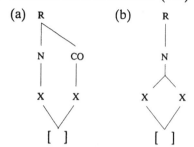

It will be assumed that the vowels associate to x slots with a syllable head. The constraint shown below says that if an x slot has a syllable head, it cannot have [−voc] content.

(235) VOCALIC ASSOCIATION CONSTRAINT (VAC)

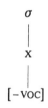

If at some point in the derivation an x slot loses its syllable head association, then it also loses its [+voc] content. The VOCALIC DELINKING RULE states that if a syllable head is pruned, the [+voc] content is delinked. PRUNING here is indicated by encircling the syllable head and it's accompanying association line.

(236) VOCALIC DELINKING (VD)

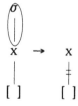

Coda constraint. Shilluk syllables are typically HEAVY syllables. A heavy syllable, as defined by Hyman (1985a) may be vc or vv or in other terminology, a heavy syllable is a syllable whose rime branches. As we have seen, in most Shilluk words, the rime does branch into a nucleus and a coda. As such, the norm for Shilluk words is to have a heavy syllable (cvc).

In the case of a word with the structure cvvc, it is considered to be a SUPERHEAVY syllable. The rime structure is vvc. It is not possible to have vcc in the rime of a Shilluk syllable.

From the perspective of the syllable templates, the claims being made for Shilluk are (1) that the nucleus can branch, but only in marked (lexically specified) cases, and (2) codas cannot branch. Evidence for these claims will be discussed shortly.

The BRANCHING CODA CONSTRAINT says that it is not permissible for a coda to branch.

(237) BRANCHING CODA CONSTRAINT (BCC)

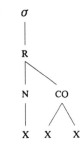

In the event that a branching coda could arise in the course of a derivation, there needs to be a principle to govern the syllabification process. Shilluk seems to have chosen a principle of rightmost selection in the case of codas. In other words, given two or more unsyllabified x slots, the rightmost slot will be the one to be syllabified.

(238) CODA SYLLABIFICATION (RIGHTMOST SELECTION) PRINCIPLE (CSP)

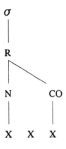

Finally, if an x slot is left unsyllabified, then the feature matrix of the segment will ultimately receive no phonetic realization. This unsyllabified segment delinking convention is shown in (239).

(239) SEGMENT DELINKING CONVENTION (SDC)

Following Haraguchi (1987), Michaels (1987) and Noske (1987), syllabification constraints will control the inclusion or exclusion of timing elements within Shilluk words. In order to show how syllable structure functions, it will be necessary to show forms in the underlying representation which are not considered ALLOWED or PROPER forms. The CODA SYLLABIFICATION PRINCIPLE will be employed to correct the form into an ALLOWABLE or syllabified structure. In this way, we will see how important syllabification is in Shilluk. Instead of devising ad hoc rules to account for various vowel and consonant insertions or deletions, syllabification rules will provide a simple, consistent means for explaining numerous irregularities in Shilluk.

4.5. Application of syllable structure

We now want to apply the syllabification procedures and constraints to underlying forms. Most of the examples are nouns since they are often inflected. Verbs have the same type of syllable structure, but are not inflected. They will be included to show FORM A and FORM B, but without any inflections.

There are three varieties of words distinguished by the length of the root vowel. Within the root of INVARIABLY SHORT VOWEL (IS) words is a single vowel which shows no long vowel in any other forms. These words contrast with INVARIABLY LONG (IL) and ALTERNATINGLY SHORT AND LONG VOWEL (ASL) words discussed in §4.5.

It will be recalled from chapter 3 that there are two types of semantically singular nouns. The neutral form was referred to as singular (SG) while the morphologically marked form was referred to as a singulative (SGLT). The semantically plural words also have morphologically marked and unmarked forms (plural (PL) and collective (COLL), respectively).

As words are introduced for derivation, the morphemic structure (μ) will be shown. However, in subsequent steps and subsequent uses of the same example word, that particular aspect of structure will be omitted. In general, only the relevant morphemic structure will be indicated.

Invariably short vowel words. Below we see invariably short vowel words from both the singular and singulative sets. Given alongside the citation form is the word with the possessive marker -ē 'his/hers/its' and also with the referential determiner -ání 'this'. Some examples of FORM A and FORM B verbs are also included.

(240) SG   SG + PS   SG + ání

   cye̱w   ———   cye̱wání   'porcupine'
   àbôn   àbónē   àbónání   'pastor'
   dítwɔ̱l   dítwɔ̱lē   dítwɔ̱lání   'black and white bull'

(241) SGLT   SGLT + PS   SGLT + ání

   àkèlɔ̀   àkèl:ē   àkèl:ání   'kind of food'
   dɔ̱ŋɔ̱   dɔ̱ŋ:ē   dɔ̱ŋ:ání   'basket'
   àbṵrɔ̀   àbṵr:ē   àbṵr:ání   'reedbuck'

(242) FORM A   FORM B

   ku̱m   ku̱mɔ   'to cover'
   ke̱t   ke̱dɔ   'to go'
   dic   dijɔ   'to lock'

We assume the syllable heads to be indicated underlyingly. The relevant morphemes are also shown. In order to syllabify the various words shown, we first associate the x slot to the left for the onset. If there is a consonant + glide sequence, then two x slots would be associated to the onset. Then, the x slot to the right is associated to the coda or internal rime structure so that the resulting structure conforms to the syllable templates allowed in Shilluk. In both cases the process is very straightforward.

(243)

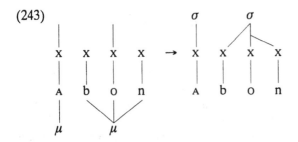

Shilluk Phonology

(244)

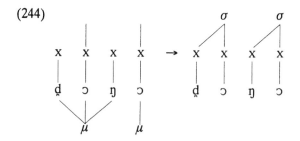

Alternatingly short and long vowel words. Alternatingly short and long vowel words are the largest set of words.

(245) SG   SG + PS   SG + ání

     pàm   pà:mē   pà:mání   'sawn timber'
     káŋ   ká:ŋē   ká:ŋání   'trumpet'
     ṭwɔ̱l   ṭwɔ̱:lē   ṭwɔ̱:láni   'snake'

(246) SGLT   SGLT + PS   SGLT + ání

     byè:lɔ́   byèl:ē   byèl:ání   'millet'
     cī:nɔ̱   cīn:ē   cīn:ání   'intestine'
     dwà̱:lɔ́   dwà̱l:ē   dwà̱l:ání   'fat'

(247) FORM A   FORM B

     bak   ba̱:gɔ   'to boil'
     bak   ba̱:gɔ   'to fence'
     ra̱p   ra̱:bɔ   'to burn'

We find that in SG words, the root vowel is short in the citation form but long in the inflected forms. By contrast, in the SGLT forms, the root vowel is long in the citation form but becomes short in modified forms with the appearance of a geminate root-final consonant. We will examine each group individually beginning with an example from the SG set. The leftmost segment of the head is preassociated, but the other is not. Since codas cannot branch, the string is syllabified according to the CODA SYLLABIFICATION PRINCIPLE. The coda is associated to the unsyllabified x slot which is farthest from the syllable head. In this case, the penultimate x slot is left unassociated, and thus will not appear on the surface.

(248)

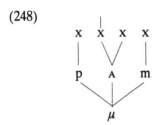

According to our syllable structure hierarchy of §4.3, template (228a) for CVC or CVV words is the expected pattern rather than (228b) for CVV or CVVC. The use of the (228b) template will be dealt with in §4.5. For the present, we will choose the more common template and attempt to syllabify the string.

(249)

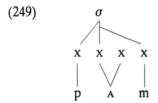

We see that one of the posthead x slots cannot be syllabified. As a result, the CODA SYLLABIFICATION PRINCIPLE is applied to syllabify the coda.

(250)

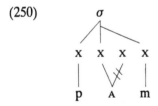

The segment attached to the unsyllabified x slot cannot surface by the SEGMENT DELINKING CONVENTION. The result is the correct surface form [pam].

(251)

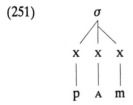

Shilluk Phonology

The presence of a word-final vowel in the SGLT words allows the syllabification process to proceed without any problems (252).

(253)

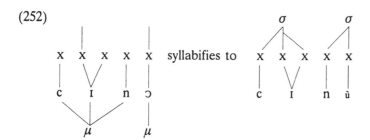

Here the coda slot syllabifies the second vowel slot since the [n], in this case, is the onset of the second syllable. The c_2 becomes the onset of the second syllable. The second slot of the vowel is syllabified as the coda. All segments surface.

While these examples are fresh in our minds, let us look at inflected forms such as the possessive marker (PS) and the referential determiner (RD). We will find in chapter 5 that the number marker (NM) has special significance to the phonology and must be handled separately from the other inflections. The inflected SG words create no problems since they end in a vowel. Below are examples from both the invariably short vowel words and the alternatingly short and long vowel words.

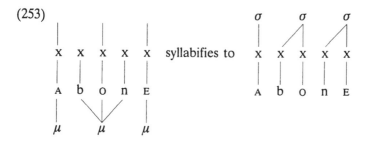

As we look at the ASL vowel words, we see that the inflected form has none of the complications of the citation form of the word. The root-final consonant has become the onset of the next syllable and the second root vowel fits into the coda slot. As a result, there is no unsyllabified element.

(254)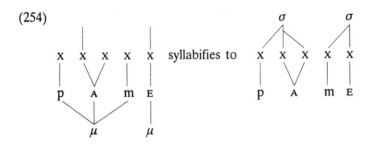

Noske (1982:274) suggests that syllabification is persistent. His hypothesis states that once syllabification has applied, resyllabification takes place persistently. We will see, not only in the current example, but also in the succeeding ones that this hypothesis is upheld.

Perhaps the clearest application of the persistent syllabification process is seen with words ending in a vowel. In this situation, a word level constraint comes into play. In Shilluk, two distinct syllable heads may not occur together without an intervening consonant.

(255) PHONOLOGICAL WORD LEVEL CONSTRAINT (PWL)

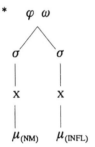

When, in the course of a derivation, this PHONOLOGICAL WORD LEVEL CONSTRAINT is violated, the DUAL SYLLABLE HEAD PRUNING RULE is implemented to make the structure syllabifiable.

Shilluk Phonology

(256) DUAL SYLLABLE HEAD PRUNING RULE (DSHP)

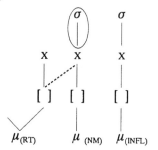

The DSHP prevents the disallowed structure of two contiguous syllable heads by pruning the leftmost syllable head. The [+VOC] features that have been associated to the x slot with the syllable head (235) must be delinked because the structure for defining a vowel is no longer present (236). It is important to note that the x slot is not lost. Instead, the feature matrix from the preceding x slot is allowed to spread onto that slot. Shilluk normally implements left to right spreading.

Let us look at *ɖɔŋɔ + e* 'his basket'.

(257)

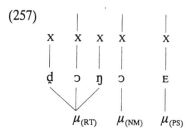

From the example shown here, it is apparent that the PHONOLOGICAL WORD LEVEL CONSTRAINT, (255), will be violated. When two syllable heads come together at the word level, the leftmost one is pruned. However, the timing slot is not lost even though the [+VOC] content is delinked. Instead, the root-final consonant spreads left to right (L→R) onto that slot resulting in a geminate consonant. The end result is a CVC+CV pattern.

Shilluk Syllable Structure

(258)

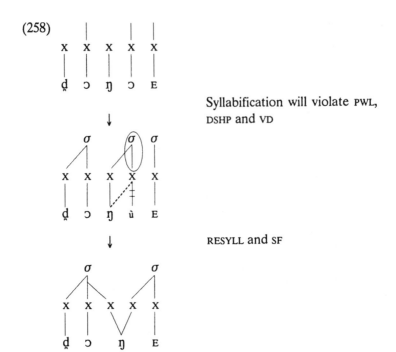

Syllabification will violate PWL, DSHP and VD

RESYLL and SF

When considering the alternatingly short and long vowel words, there is a slightly more complicated situation. We return to a previous example, this time with a possessive inflection, $c\underline{i}{:}n\underline{\mathfrak{o}}+e$ 'his intestine'. First, we have the partially syllabified underlying representation.

(259)

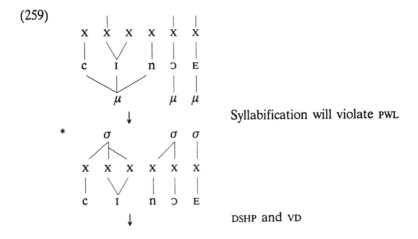

Syllabification will violate PWL

DSHP and VD

Shilluk Phonology

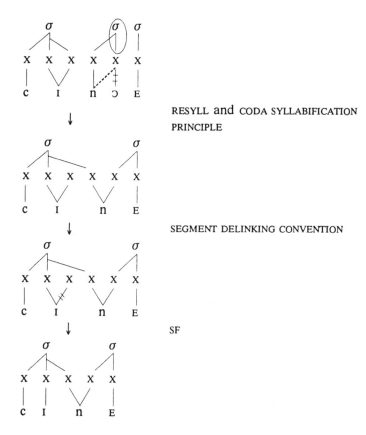

The DUAL SYLLABLE HEAD PRUNING RULE eliminates the SGLT (NM) suffix and allows for the doubling of the root-final consonant. The resulting form must be resyllabified. The CODA SYLLABIFICATION PRINCIPLE applies and leaves the second vowel unsyllabified. Since it cannot be syllabified, it cannot surface.

It may appear that a lot of fuss is being made over a simple vowel truncation rule that shortens a vowel in a closed syllable. However, there is more to this problem, for now we must account for words which remain long under all conditions.

Invariably long vowel words. In the words given below, we see that the vowel in the root is long and remains so in the inflected forms. Notice also that there is no gemination of the root-final consonant since both geminate vowels and consonants may not occur in a single root. If a geminate consonant occurred, then the coda would branch and that structure is not allowed in Shilluk.

118   Shilluk Syllable Structure

(260) SG   SG + PS   SG + ání

       ágɔ̄:l   ágɔ̄:lē   ágɔ̄:lání   'scarecrow'
       bù:r   bù:rē   bù:rání   'grave'
       gɔ̄:l   gɔ̄:lē   gɔ̄:lání   'wild dog'

(261) SGLT   SGLT + PS   SGLT + ání

       àdè:rɔ̀   àdè:rē   àdè:rání   'donkey'
       gɔ̄:lɔ̄   gɔ̄:lē   gɔ̄:lání   'hook'
       dɔ̄:lɔ̄   dɔ̄:lē   dɔ̄:lání   'ring of grass'

(262) FORM A   FORM B

       kwa:n   kwa̠:n   'to count'
       cwɔ:ŋ   cwɔ:ŋ   'to delay'
       ma:r   ma̠:t   'to love'

It is interesting that these words *never* have a root-final geminate. It is
as though the doubled vowel had some dominant characteristic such that
the vowel stays intact while the EXTRA consonant is not allowed phonetic
realization. Certainly in the alternatingly short and long words, the vowel
is shortened in a closed syllable and a root-final consonant may geminate.
With the invariably long vowel words, the vowel has precedence. For this
reason, it seems logical to reflect this difference in the syllable structure.
Thus template (228b) is suggested.

Words of this type constitute a much smaller class. The assumption here
is that they are marked in the underlying representation as words which
have a complex nucleus so that both vowels are preassociated with a single
nucleus. In no case can either vowel be delinked. This set of words is
referred to as the INVARIABLY LONG VOWEL words and each must be marked
in the underlying representation as being of this type.

We have seen in our syllable hierarchy that CVVC syllables of this type
are the most marked. We need to add a qualifier to this template to
indicate that the full form (CVVC) may only occur word finally.

Shilluk Phonology

(263) MARKED VOWEL CODA CONSTRAINT (MVCC)

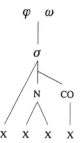

Returning now, to the syllabification of invariably long vowel words, we have the following process.

(264)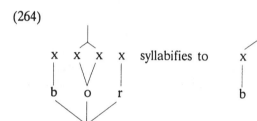

(265)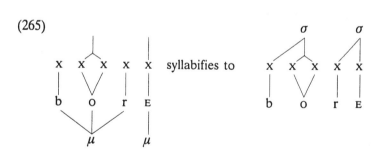

120　　　　　　　　　　　　　　　　　　　Shilluk Syllable Structure

Similarly,

(266)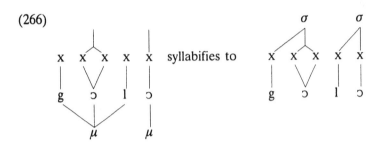

When we begin to examine the inflected form of the SGLT, we find an interesting development in the derivation. In previous examples with alternatingly short and long vowel words, we saw that geminate consonants were accommodated by fitting the first consonant into the coda slot (via the CODA SYLLABIFICATION PRINCIPLE) and the second into the onset of the next syllable. However, with invariably long vowel words, this arrangement is not acceptable. Geminate vowels and consonants cannot co-occur in the same root since this would violate the constraint in (255). The solution to this incompatible situation is to delink the coda slot. The CODA DELINKING RULE is given below.

(267) MARKED VOWEL CODA DELINKING (MVCD)

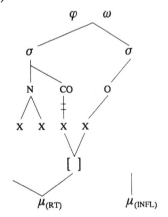

The MARKED VOWEL CODA DELINKING rule applies to syllables with a branching or marked nucleus. If in the course of the derivation, a geminate consonant arises, the coda must be delinked. Then the segmental feature matrix

Shilluk Phonology

is delinked from the timing tier by the SEGMENT DELINKING CONVENTION; thus allowing the structure to be properly syllabified. Below we see how this rule applies in a SGLT word with a possessive inflection.

(268)

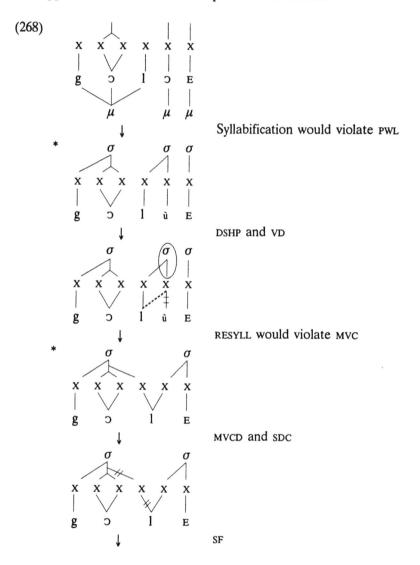

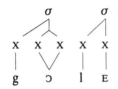

Comparison of two cvv templates. Let us look again at the two templates for a cvv syllable structure set up in §4.2.

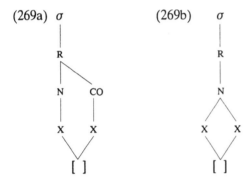

In the structure shown above, both (269a) and (269b) have cvv patterns. We know from previous discussion that (269a) will often surface as a short vowel. However, if there is no c_2 in the syllable, the vowel assigned to the two x slots will surface as a long vowel. Likewise, if the phonological word ends in a vowel, then the root vowel will surface as a long vowel. Only when the phonological word ends in a consonant or is followed by a cv syllable will the root vowel surface as a short vowel.

By contrast, the vowel in (269b) will always surface as a long vowel which cannot be shortened in any context. There is no way to predict the occurrence of words with the syllable structure shown in (269b). Therefore, it is necessary to indicate the syllable structure of these invariably long vowels in the underlying representation.

Further evidence. In §4.5, it was mentioned that the syllable pattern cvvc could only occur word finally. This string is also the maximum allowed in a Shilluk syllable. Therefore, it would not be unreasonable to expect the system to feel a bit strained at this point, and in fact, it does. Consider the following words.

Shilluk Phonology 123

(270)   + ání

ŋụ̀:   ŋụ̀:rání   'lion'
kī: kī:rání   'Nile River'
cụ̄:   cụ̄:rání   'bones'
kụ̀:   kụ̀:rání   'thief'

Note that in the citation form there is no final consonant. Yet, when these words are inflected, the root-final consonant [r] appears. While the final consonant in these words is consistently [r], they are in contrast to words which maintain the final [r], but have a different syllable structure such as: *cur* 'type of catfish (PL)', and *anir* 'scum from water'.

Presumably, the underlying structure for a word like [ŋụ̀:] is /ŋuur/ (the plural is [ŋúr:ị̄]). However, the CVVC syllable structure reduces to a simpler CVV. Again, we see that the vowel length is retained rather than allowing the final consonant to surface.

But why does this occur only with a root-final segment which is [+VIB]? The answer to that lies partly in the fact that in some dialects the [+VIB] is no longer a distinct phoneme. In these dialects the [+VIB] phoneme merged with the [+RND,+VOC] glide. Perhaps this weakening of the phonemic status in certain dialects is generally indicative that it is a less stable consonant. Perhaps such an intrinsically weak segment combined with the complexity of a CVVC syllable structure results in a loss of the c_2 when the c_2 is [+VIB]. The same pressure would not be present in a word with the (269a) structure. Thus, the [+VIB] surfaces in those words (in the majority of dialects where it is still a phoneme). In the inflected form, the final c survives because it can fit into the onset slot of the following syllable. Thus, if a superheavy syllable reduction process were to be under-way, the [+VIB] segment would be a logical place to begin. We may conclude, then, that these words offer us some further evidence that our hypothesis for a second type of syllable template which is phonologically marked may be valid.

4.6. Plural forms

Up to this point, we have only dealt with singular and singulative words. Now we take up the plural words which for the most part, make use of the same rules as the singulars just discussed. Plurals, however, will need to be dealt with independently since they are not derivable from singulars. Derivations of (or rather the inability to derive) singular/plural words have been dealt with in more detail in chapter 3. Further evidence for this claim of independent underlying representations will be made in this chapter.

The term collective (COLL) will be used for the morphologically unmarked plural form as it relates to its semantic function and is more easily distinguished from the morphologically marked plural (PL).

Collective words. Collective words in Shilluk usually have the shape CVC. Like the SG forms, COLL words are neutral with regard to number; they have no number suffix. In most cases, COLL words have a SGLT counterpart.

In the SGLT forms of nouns, we saw that geminate consonants appeared as part of the derivation. However, for these COLL words, it would seem necessary to posit a root-final geminate in the underlying representation (271).

(271) UR   SR
                COLL   COLL+PS   COLL+ání
       /byell/ byél   byél:é   byél:ání   'millet'
       /ciŋŋ/   cíŋ   cíŋ:é   cíŋ:ání   'hand'
       /alebb/ álèp   álèp:é   álèp:ání   'African darter'

Upon examination of the data, we see one CVC form (in the citation form) and one CVCC inflected form. The reader may recall that in the derivation of an inflected SGLT word (258), the -ɔ suffix was delinked and the root-final consonant was allowed to spread to that x slot. The phonetic realization is a root-final geminate consonant. It would simplify the analysis if a similar sort of derivation could be set up for the COLL words. However, since COLL words have no number suffix, there is nothing from which to derive a root-final geminate. Given this situation, it seems necessary to posit a root-final geminate in the underlying representation. When syllabification applies, the CODA SYLLABIFICATION PRINCIPLE will assign the coda to the final unassociated x slot. The penultimate x slot will not appear on the surface since any unsyllabified element cannot have a phonetic realization. The result is a single root-final consonant word finally, but a geminate root-final consonant intervocalically (272).

(272)

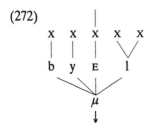

Syllabification would violate BCC, CSP

Shilluk Phonology 125

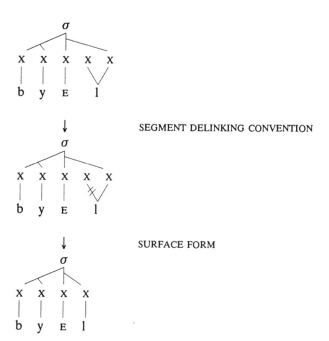

Having allowed for the root-final geminate in the underlying representation, syllabifying the inflected form presents no difficulty.

(273)

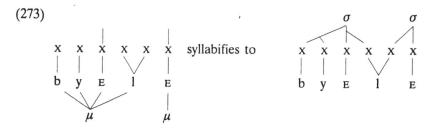

As innocent as this solution may appear, we will find that the implications are striking. If this analysis is accepted, then the underlying representations for singular and plural are structurally different. The SGLT, in this case, has a single root-final consonant while the COLL has a geminate root-final consonant. Let us consider the two together.

(274) COLL   COLL+PS   SGLT   SGLT+PS
     byel   *byel:e*   *bye:lɔ* *byel:e*   'millet'

126   Shilluk Syllable Structure

Without the geminate in the underlying representation of the COLL, we
see the following derivation.

(275)

COLL	COLL + PS	SGLT	SGLT + PS	
/byEEl/	/byEEl + E/	/byEEl + ɔ/	/byEEl + ɔ + E/	
———	———	———	byeelle	DSHP
byel	———	———	byelle	CSP
[byel]	*[bye:le]	[bye:lɔ]	[byel:e]	SF

We see that there is no way to get a geminate consonant in the inflected
COLL form without positing its presence in the underlying representation.
As a result of failing to posit such a structure, the root vowel remains long
when it should be shortened.

If the geminate is posited in both COLL and SGLT, we see further
problems.

(276)

COLL	COLL + PS	SGLT	SGLT + PS	
/byEEll/	/byEEll + E/	/byEEll + ɔ/	/byEEll + ɔ + E/	
———	———	———	byeelle	DSHP
byel	byelle	byellɔ	byelle	CSP
[byel]	[byel:e]	*[byel:ɔ]	[byel:e]	SF

If the root-final geminate is in both forms, then it ought to appear in the
citation form of the SGLT, which is incorrect.

If, however, we allow for this structural difference between SGLT and
COLL, the derivation works satisfactorily. It will be recalled that such a
conclusion is independently motivated on account of substantial differences
between the two root forms which, it was claimed, present insuperable
problems to morpheme invariance (see §§3.2 and 3.3).

(277)

COLL	COLL + PS	SGLT	SGLT + PS	
/byEEll/	/byEEll + E/	/byEEl + ɔ/	/byEEl + ɔ + E/	
———	———	———	byeelle	DSHP
byel	byelle	———	byelle	CSP
[byel]	[byel:e]	[bye:lɔ]	[byel:e]	SF

Thus, we see that a root-final geminate needs to be posited in the
underlying representation for COLL words, but *not* posited for the SGLT
words. This further evidence for the claim of independent underlying

Shilluk Phonology

representations does not stop here, however. We move on now to the plural words.

Plurals with -*i* suffix. In contrast to the COLL words discussed above, there are plural (PL) words. These words typically have an -*i* suffix as a plural marker. They often have a SG counterpart, but may have a SGLT in some cases.

The pattern of these PL words is to have a geminate root-final consonant and the -*i* plural marker in the citation form (278).

(278) PL   PL+PS   PL+*ání*
       pám:į̄   *pám:é*   *pàm:ání*   'sawn timber'
       lą̂n:į̀   *lą̂n:é*   *lą̂n:ání*   'chieftainship'
       ṭól:ī   *ṭól:é*   *ṭól:ání*   'snake'

Presumably the underlying representation would be similar to the COLL form with a root-final geminate. The PL, however, would also include the -*i* suffix. The derivation would look as in (279).

(279) /pAmm+I/   /pAmm+I+E/
       ———   *pammme   DSHP
       ———   pamme   CSP
       [pạm:į]   [pạm:e]   SF

In the course of the derivation, the delinking of the -*i* suffix (as a result of DUAL SYLLABLE HEAD PRUNING) could be assumed to prune the syllable head associated with the plural suffix. The plural suffix would then be delinked and the root-final consonant allowed to spread to that x slot. However, in the syllabification process, the CODA SYLLABIFICATION PRINCIPLE would only allow two of those consonants to surface. The third could not be syllabified and thus would receive no phonetic realization.

(280)

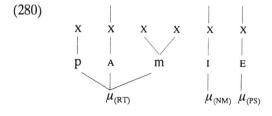

↓   Syllabification would violate PWL

128   Shilluk Syllable Structure

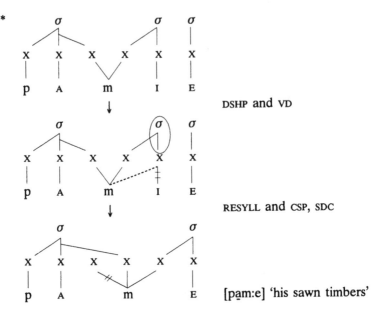

It is not clear whether the underlying representation has a double vowel (alternatingly short and long) or an invariably short vowel. By comparison with the singular words there seems to be a significant difference in the frequency of occurrence between ASL and IS. In the singulars, most words come from the ASL set. However, in the plural, most words seem to come from the IS set. One explanation for this could be that both ASL and IS words surface as single vowels because of the gemination of the final consonant. The ASL words are then automatically reduced or simplified, thus giving the impression that plural words have a significantly higher proportion of IS words. As can be seen from the derivations below, the result is the same with either analysis.

(281) /pAAmm+ɪ/   or   /pAmm+ɪ/   UR
       pAmmɪ   ———   CSP
       [pam:i]   [pam:i]   SF

We come again to the question of an underlying representation for SG and PL words. If we assume, for the sake of convenience, that both SG and PL forms have an ASL vowel in the root, we would *still* need to allow for a doubled root-final consonant in the PL form. Consider the alternatives.

Shilluk Phonology   129

(282) SG   SG+PS   PL   PL+PS
      pàm   pà:mē   pám:ī   pám:é   'sawn timber'

We have the following derivation without the root-final geminate.

(283) SG   SG+PS   PL   PL+PS
      /pʌʌm/   /pʌʌm+ɛ/   /pʌʌm+ɪ/   /pʌʌm+ɪ+ɛ/   UR
      ─────   ─────   ─────   *pʌʌmmɛ   DSHP
      pʌm   ─────   ─────   pʌmmɛ   CSP
      [pạm]   [pạ:me]   *[pạ:mị]   [pạm:e]   SF

The PL form is incorrect because there is no root-final geminate. Further, since there is no geminate consonant, the syllable is open and the vowel remains long.
If we include the root-final geminate in both forms, the reverse problem appears.

(284) SG   SG+PS   PL   PL+PS
      /pʌʌmm/   /pʌʌmm+ɛ/   /pʌʌmm+ɪ/   /pʌʌmm+ɪ+ɛ/   UR
      ─────   ─────   ─────   *pʌʌmmmɛ   DSHP
      pʌm   pʌmmɛ   pʌmmɪ   pʌmmɛ   CSP
      [pạm]   *[pạm:e]   [pạm:ị]   [pạm:e]   SF

The geminate in the inflected SG form reduces the vowel and leaves the geminate consonant resulting in an incorrect form. The point at issue here is that, two distinct results must be achieved given identical syllable patterns. We must recognize this requirement as impossible unless there is an underlying structural difference between them. The conclusion, then, is that the PL has a root-final geminate consonant which is not present in the SG.

(285) SG   SG+PS   PL   PL+PS
      /pʌʌm/   /pʌʌm+ɛ/   /pʌʌmm+ɪ/   /pʌʌmm+ɪ+ɛ/   UR
      ─────   ─────   ─────   *pʌʌmmmɛ   DSHP
      pʌm   ─────   ─────   ─────   CSP
      [pạm]   [pạ:mē]   [pạm:ī]   [pạm:é]   SF

One other solution to this dilemma seems possible. Perhaps the plural marking is $c+i$. The c would be unspecified and would take on the feature matrix of the root-final consonant. This solution would provide the necessary structure for a correct derivation. Only one problem remains, viz., the

130   Shilluk Syllable Structure

COLL words are unmarked for PL and yet a geminate consonant is present in the underlying representation. Without positing different underlying representations for COLL and PL words, this solution does not seem to be viable. It is unlikely that geminate-final consonants are present only in COLL words and are added as a PL marker in all the other plural nouns.

Thus, it seems we are forced to posit a geminate root-final consonant in the plural words whether morphologically marked (PL) or unmarked (COLL). This geminate consonant is not to be found in the underlying representation of the singular nouns. Once that basic assumption is in place, the rules are quite orderly and systematic. Without the two forms, confusion reigns. So, as my predecessors advised, it is necessary to learn both underlying "singular" and "plural" forms and then one can more easily become "acquainted with the rules governing the regular nouns" (Anon. 1935).

Derived plurals. The next set of words under consideration are the derived plurals.

(286)   PL   PL + PS   PL + *ání*
       gɔ̀:r   *gɔ̄r:é*   *gɔ̄r:ání*   'honey badger'
       yḕ:p   *yēp:é*   *yēp:ání*   'tail'
       bā̰:k   *bā̰k:é*   *bā̰k:ání*   'garden'

The older plural process is root + *i*. However, there seems to be a movement within Nilotic languages toward becoming monosyllabic. Dinka has already become almost exclusively monosyllabic. And, at least within the plural formation, Shilluk is also losing suffixes. This process is currently in progress and some dialects, age groups, etc. choose one rule and some the other for forming plurals. Some people argue with themselves over which way sounds RIGHT for a particular word.

One Shilluk has reported to me that children learning the language will use the root + *i* for plurals on every word. Furthermore, he said that as they grow older, they use the alternative form as described by the metathesis rule given below. While I have not been able to personally observe this behavior, it would be an interesting confirmation for this hypothesis.

The PLURAL -I INCORPORATION RULE or METATHESIS RULE is optional, depending on the factors mentioned above. It could be hypothesized that there is a metathesis rule which moves the plural -*i* marker into the nucleus of the root. In the process, it changes the syllable structure of that form so as to create the marked long vowel (i.e., with complex nucleus).

Shilluk Phonology

(287) (optional) PLURAL METATHESIS RULE (PMR)

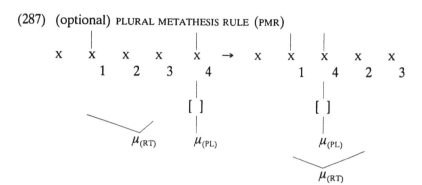

It is interesting to note that this monosyllabification process occurs with the -*i* suffix in plural words. Later (§4.7), we will see the same process with the -*i* suffix in the verbs. Since it seems that there is a consistently motivated series of steps at work here, we should examine it more closely.

The process of monosyllabification or I-INCORPORATION, as it will be termed in this thesis, is composed of several steps. First of all, the x slot associated with the plural number marker is moved into the root so that it is contiguous to the root vowel. This movement can be shown on the vowel plane as follows.

(288) SYLLABLE HEAD MOVEMENT (SHM)

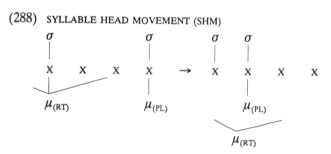

After SHM has occurred, the two vowels are united into a complex nucleus by means of Chomsky adjunction. I will call this step NUCLEAR ADJUNCTION.

(289) NUCLEAR ADJUNCTION (NA)

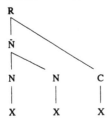

This results in a complex nucleus.

(290)

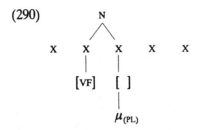

In chapter 2, the maximally underspecified vowel for Shilluk was said to be [i]. Since this vowel would normally receive no feature content until the final stages of the derivation, it is not surprising that, in the course of adjunction, this unspecified segment takes on the features of the root-vowel with which it is joined. This assimilation process is shown in (291).

(291) ROOT VOWEL SPREADING RULE (RVSR)

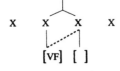

Viewing the I-INCORPORATION PROCESS (IIP) in this way eliminates the need for the Metathesis Rule. Furthermore, it explains why this process *only* occurs with the [i] vowel since the I's maximally underspecified status makes it the best candidate for a total assimilation to the root vowel. Through this process, we can also see that the morphological information of the *-i* suffix is retained in the word (by means of the long root vowel) even though the suffix *per se* is no longer present. Finally, the IIP explains why there is a long vowel in a closed syllable in alternatingly short and long words which typically cannot have that combination.

Shilluk Phonology

In chapter 5, we will see that the number marker receives its [EX] value from the root vowel. As such, we would not expect to have any [EX] feature change as a result of the IIP, and in fact, there is no change of the [EX] feature resulting from the process. The tone on the plural marker, however, is incorporated into the root. One speaker gave the following two alternatives for the plural of 'grasshopper': bâ:ɲ ~ bâɲ:i̧.

Thus, instead of losing the tone or having a floating tone, the incorporated vowel moves the tone into the root along with the syllable head. Therefore, the IIP would seem to offer an explanation for the unusually high number of instances of tone sequences in derived plural words. For a further discussion of tone in derived plurals see §5.1.

In conclusion, we have now seen two ways in which contiguous syllable heads are dealt with in Shilluk. First, if the number suffix and another inflection are involved, the DUAL SYLLABLE HEAD PRUNING RULE is implemented, ultimately resulting in a root-final geminate consonant. On the other hand, if the number suffix is moved into the root (IIP), the result is a change in syllable structure which produces an INVARIABLY LONG vowel in the citation form of the plural.

In the derivation given below, the steps of the I-INCORPORATION PROCESS are shown. Once IIP has applied, the CODA SYLLABIFICATION PRINCIPLE will fail to syllabify one of the root-final geminate consonants. The SEGMENT DELINKING CONVENTION will prevent it from appearing on the surface. It will be shown in §5.1 that the IIP is implemented at a late stage. Therefore, the inflected form is unaffected by the IIP process.

(292)

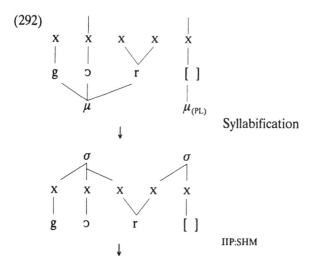

Shilluk Syllable Structure

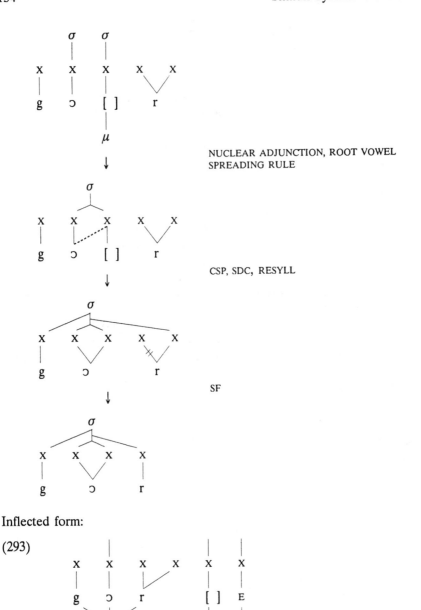

NUCLEAR ADJUNCTION, ROOT VOWEL SPREADING RULE

CSP, SDC, RESYLL

SF

Inflected form:

(293)

Syllabification would violate PWL

Shilluk Phonology

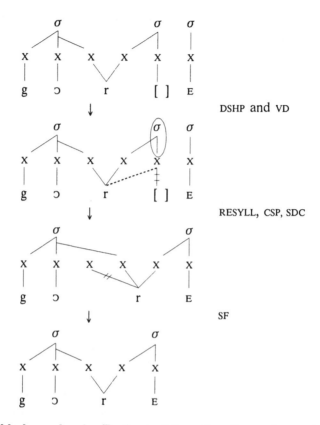

Invariably long plurals. Earlier in this section, it was shown that alternatingly short and long words and invariably short vowel words appear to be identical on the surface. These words stand in contrast to the IL vowel words discussed here. From our discussion of SGLT words, we recall that gemination of consonants may not co-occur with the IL vowels. Consider (294) and (295).

(294)   PL   PL+PS   PL+*ání*
        kwệ:rị   *kwệ:ré*   *kwệ:ráni*   'small hoe'
        bộ:tị̀   ————   *bộ:táni*   'craftsman'

(295)   PL   PL+PS   PL+*ání*
        cɔ̀:r   ————   *cɔ̀:ráni*   'blind person'
        ápè:d   *ápè:dé*   *ápè:dáni*   'skunk'
        dụ́:p   ————   *dụ́:páni*   'swamp rat'

136   Shilluk Syllable Structure

The root vowel is assumed in these cases to be marked as a long vowel.
The derivations would involve the MARKED VOWEL CODA DELINKING RULE
which eliminates the first of the geminate root-final consonants.

(296) /kwEEɪr + ɪ/   /kwEEɪr + ɪ + E/   UR
      ─────   *kweerrre   DSHP, VD
      kweeri   kweere   MVCD, SDC
      [kweːri]   [kweːre]   SF

(297) /cɔɔrr/   /cɔɔrr + ʌnɪ/   UR
      cɔɔr   ─────   CSP, SDC
      ─────   cɔɔrani   MVCD, SDC
      [cɔːr]   [cɔːrani]   SF

The geminate consonant posited in the underlying representation is a
fairly abstract entity since it never surfaces with these words. However, as
root-final consonant gemination appears to be a consistent feature of
plural, it seems reasonable to include it by analogy with invariably short
words and alternatingly short and long words.

Morphemic status for templates and syllable structure. In our discussion of nouns, we saw that the semantically singular forms have a
root-final consonant while the semantically plural forms have a root-final
geminate consonant. Within the framework of the nonlinear model, the
timing tier or prosodic template is the tier into which this morphological
information is coded. The c and v tiers simply attach to the appropriate x
slots by UNIVERSAL ASSOCIATION CONVENTIONS. Thus, we may conclude that
the prosodic template has morphemic status as was claimed by McCarthy
(1982). In Shilluk, then, the extra x slot to which the root-final consonant
attaches signals that that form is semantically plural.

It is also suggested that syllable structure may have morphemic status. In
the previous sections, it was shown that virtually nothing is predictable
between the singular and plural forms of a word. However, nothing was
said specifically about syllable structure. In fact, syllable structure cannot
be predicted either. While the syllable structure often seems to be the
same between FORM A and FORM B, there are instances where one of them
(usually the semantically singular) will have an invariably long vowel and
the other (usually the semantically plural) will have either an invariably
short or alternatingly short and long vowel as in (297).

Shilluk Phonology

(298)
SG	SG+ání	PL	PL+ání	
áyē:r	áyē:rání	áyēr:ì	áyēr:ání	'curlew bird'
átê:gɔ̀	átê:ŋání	átè:k	átèk:ání	'goat'
bù:r	bù:rání	būr	būr:ání	'grave'
cò:gɔ̀	cò:ŋání	cōk	cōk:ání	'eel-like catfish'

The SGLT forms, if they were alternatingly short and long vowel words or invariably short vowel words, would have a geminate root-final consonant in the inflected form. However, we see that these words do not have a geminate consonant. Instead, the vowel stays long in both the citation and inflected forms. On the other hand, the plural forms of those words conform to the patterns expected for ASL and IS vowel words. Thus, I conclude that syllable structure also seems to have morphemic status.

4.7. Verbs and syllable structure

In chapter 3, we saw several forms of verbs. Besides active and passive, there were the FORM A and FORM B. Following (299), the verb will be examined in light of the syllable structure rules just discussed.

(299)
ja:l dwɔ̰ŋ yep:a ɖɔ ɔt	'The man opens the door.'
ɖɔ ɔt yep yḭ ja:l dwɔ̰ŋ	'The door is opened by the man.'
yá yep:a ɖɔ ɔt	'I opened the door.'
ya ye̱:p	'I opened (it).'
ya ye̱p:i̱ meya	'I opened (it) for my mother.'
ya ye̱:ba tɔŋ	'I opened (it) with a spear.'

From chapter 3, there were three word orders given for Shilluk. This discussion will concentrate on the SVCMP order.

(300)
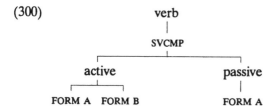

According to the conclusions drawn earlier, independent underlying representations must be posited for FORM A and FORM B. From those two forms, however, we should be able to derive other forms. Syllable structure will play an important role in our derivations.

138 Shilluk Syllable Structure

Notice that FORM A is used for both active and passive voice. FORM B allows no complement. However, we will see that, like the plurals, FORM B may come in two versions: root + -i, and an incorporated version. The discussion will show that the I-INCORPORATION PROCESS (IIP) is not limited to the nominal system, but is also used in the verbs. Finally, FORM B can be used as the basis for deriving the benefactive and instrumental verb forms.

(301)   FORM A   FORM B (with -i)   →   IIP form
         ⌜────┴────⌝   ⌜──────┴──────⌝
         active passive   benefactive instrumental

FORM A **active and passive verbs.** First, consider FORM A from which the active and passive of the SVCMP order is derived. If an alternatingly short and long vowel is posited in the underlying representation along with a root-final geminate consonant, we have the following derivations for [yep], [yep:a] 'to open'.

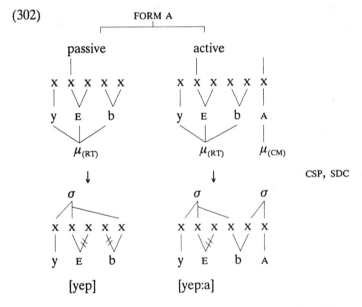

The active FORM A always has the -a complement marker. The passive form has no complement marker. Therefore, when the CODA SYLLABIFICATION PRINCIPLE applies, the surface forms are quite different, though they have a common underlying root.

In order to syllabify the passive form, the CSP must apply. In this case, one vowel and one consonant are not able to be realized phonetically since

Shilluk Phonology

they cannot be syllabified. The various POSTLEXICAL TENSING and INTERVOCALIC ASPIRATION rules would apply though the steps are not shown here.

FORM B verbs. Now, we turn our attention to FORM B. Interestingly enough, we encounter the same situation here that we did for the plural nouns. There seems to be an inconsistent I-INCORPORATION PROCESS in operation. Consider the words in (303).

(303a) FORM B
kẹt:į   '—— speared'
yẹ̄y:į   '—— answered'
gɔ̄c:į   '—— hit'
mạ̄k:į   '—— summoned'

(303b) FORM B
kyẹ̄:t   '—— fried'
wị:y   '—— left (it) alone'
gɔ̄:k   '—— worked'
bạ̄:k   '—— boiled'

There is a striking similarity between the structure of these two forms and that of the plurals. It seems that I-INCORPORATION PROCESS is at work here too, but has not yet affected all the words in the lexicon. For the derivation of these words, we may assume an alternatingly short and long vowel and geminate root-final consonant. The derivation would also work for invariably short vowel words, but the ASL words are slightly more complicated, and so were chosen for the examples.

(304)

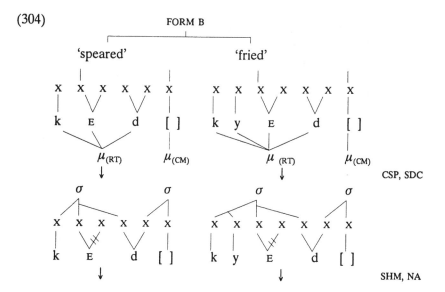

140   Shilluk Syllable Structure

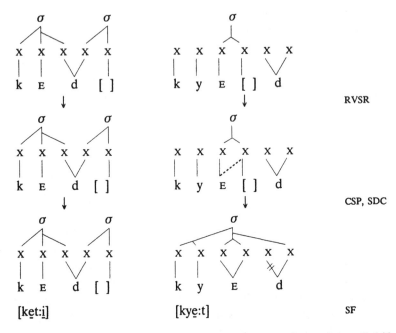

In the derivation, the CODA SYLLABIFICATION PRINCIPLE is used to syllabify the string, effectively shortening the root vowel in both forms. It will be shown in chapter 5 that I-INCORPORATION PROCESS is a later rule within the lexical level. Syllabification is assumed to be perseverative and is not specifically ordered in this derivation.

The I-INCORPORATION PROCESS involving SYLLABLE HEAD MOVEMENT and NUCLEAR ADJUNCTION takes place with (303b), but not (303a). Again, the underspecified vowel takes on the feature complex of the root vowel with which it shares a syllable head. The root-final geminate surfaces as a single consonant because of the application of the CODA SYLLABIFICATION PRINCIPLE and SEGMENT DELINKING CONVENTION. At the post-lexical level, devoicing of the plosives occurs in both words.

Benefactive verb form. The suffix -*i* indicates the benefactive form of the verb. If that -*i* is combined with FORM B suffix -*i*, then according to the rules at this point, the derivation would result in triple consonant length. Of course, by the syllabification rules for Shilluk, this triple consonant length would not be allowed to surface. The CODA SYLLABIFICATION PRINCIPLE would not syllabify one of the consonants, and thus, only two would be able to receive phonetic realization. This case in the verbs is parallel to the one in the plural nouns in §4.6.

Shilluk Phonology

There are certain elements such as tone and [EX] that are characteristic of the benefactive form. The tone on the benefactive is consistently M root tone followed by H suffix tone. This M-H sequence is not found on any other verb form of which I am aware. Therefore, it would suggest that tone has morphemic status. Furthermore, the benefactive always has [+EX] vowels (both the root and the suffix). In all the other verb forms discussed up to this point, the [EX] feature has been assigned to the vowel in the underlying representation. However, in this case, the [EX] feature seems to have morphological status since it consistently indicates the benefactive form. The remaining characteristics of the benefactive can be derived from the FORM B verb as shown in (305).

(305)

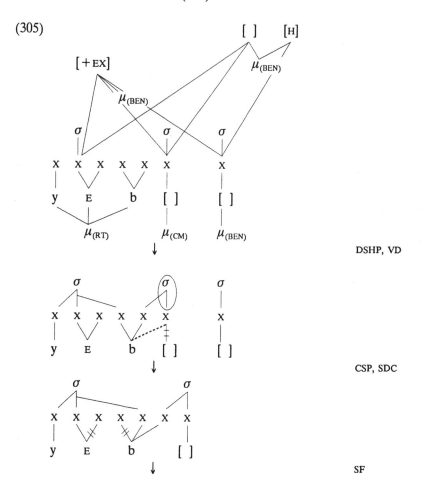

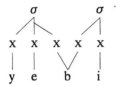 [yēp:í]

The underlying representation shows FORM B plus the -*i* benefactive suffix. The DUAL SYLLABLE HEAD PRUNING rule applies allowing the syllable head associated with the complement marker to be pruned. The vowel features are not specified since we are dealing with the non-specified segment in this case. The root-final consonant spreads, but, as with previous examples, the resulting triple consonant length is never permitted to surface. The CODA SYLLABIFICATION PRINCIPLE and the SEGMENT DELINKING CONVENTION shorten the root vowel and delink the third consonant from the timing tier. The [EX] and tone morphemes are shown on separate tiers to indicate their morphological status. At the postlexical level, the rules regarding the voicing of plosives would apply, though I have not shown those steps here.

Instrumental verb form. The characteristics peculiar to the instrumental form of the verb include a consistent [+EX] feature on the root vowel and M tone on both root and -*a* suffix. Again, the tone and [EX] features distinguish the instrumental form of the verb and thus seem to function morphologically within the representation. The -*a* suffix is always [−EX].

Structurally, the instrumental form of the verb presents a slight problem. The root vowel surfaces as a long vowel and there is a single root-final consonant. The suffix vowel is -*a*. The instrumental form is derived from the FORM B root, seen in (306).

(306)
FORM A	FORM B	INST	
ṭal	ta:t	tā:dā	'cook'
kyel	kye:t	kyē:dā	'fry'
wa:l	wa:t	wā:dā	'boil liquid'
yep	ye:p	yē:bā	'open'
ŋɔl	ŋut	ŋūtā	'cut up'

Both the consonant alternation [ṭ ~ t] and the vowel alternation [ɔ ~ u] show that the instrumental form is derived from FORM B rather than from FORM A.

So, what is the difficulty that was mentioned above? Let us examine a derivation, using the verb 'to open'.

(307)

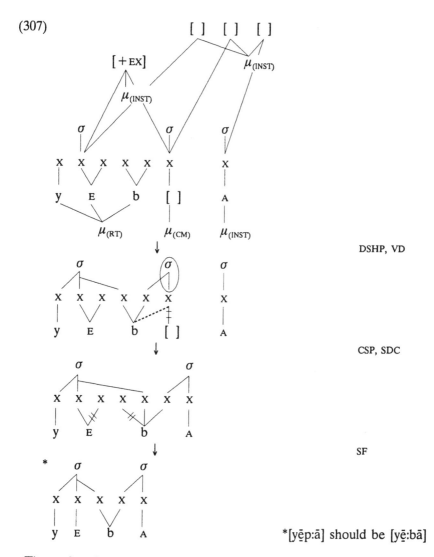

*[yẹ̃p:ā] should be [yẹ̃:bā]

The surface form has not come out as expected. The problem lies in the presence of the root-final geminate consonant. As long as the geminate is present, the CODA SYLLABIFICATION PRINCIPLE will shorten the vowel resulting in an incorrect surface form.

One alternate handling of this problem would be to omit one of the root-final consonants in the underlying representation. This solution does not really help, however, because the DUAL SYLLABLE HEAD PRUNING rule would effectively create the geminate consonant from the x slot associated with the delinked suffix vowel -*i*.

A second alternative would be to replace the -*i* suffix with the -*a* suffix. This solution is unworkable as well since the geminate consonants in the underlying representation would remain in place. The root vowel would be shortened and the problem would remain.

The third solution produces the correct result. If a root-final consonant delinking rule is introduced after the CODA SYLLABIFICATION PRINCIPLE, then the correct surface form will result. The ROOT-FINAL CONSONANT DELINKING RULE says that one of the root-final consonants is delinked and so does not receive any phonetic realization in the instrumental form of the verb.

(308) ROOT-FINAL CONSONANT DELINKING RULE (RFCDR)

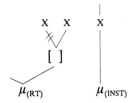

Consider the derivation in (309).

(309)

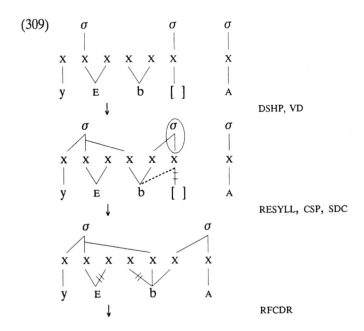

Shilluk Phonology

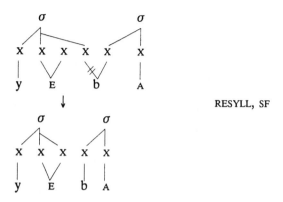

RESYLL, SF

Presumably, when the SEGMENT DELINKING CONVENTION applies, the result does not eliminate the segment from the structure. As has been seen in this derivation, if the segment can be syllabified, then it is allowed to reappear.

In order to fully discuss the derivations of the various forms of verbs, one would need to write an entire paper on that topic alone. The small section included here is intended to highlight the fact that the rules established for the nouns apply equally to the verbs. Even the I-INCORPORATION PROCESS is not solely found in plural nouns, but is a process that is also to be seen in the FORM B verb. Thus, we may conclude that there is independent confirmation in the verbal system for the syllable structure rules set up in this chapter to account for the nominal system.

4.8. Morphology

Throughout this chapter, we have seen affixes used to mark SGLT, PL, benefactive, etc. This use of affixation is common to CONCATENATIVE languages. In addition to affixation, we have seen infixation in both PL and FORM B. Further, tone and another autosegmental feature, viz. [+EX], mark the benefactive and instrumental. Such morphological features are typical of NONCONCATENATIVE languages. Since, in some cases at least, both morphological types occur in marking identical categories (e.g., plural and FORM B), we can conclude that Shilluk is in a transitional stage from being a concatenative language to becoming a nonconcatenative one.

4.9. Summary

In this chapter, we have seen that Shilluk syllable structure is one of the most powerful aspects of the phonology. There are two underlying syllable structures, one for invariably short vowel words and alternatingly short and long vowel words, and the second for invariably long vowel words.

Separate underlying representations are still required for singular and plural as well as FORM A and FORM B. It has been shown that, in addition to other differences between these forms as discussed in chapter 3, there are also underlying structural differences. For example, the plural and collective words must have a root-final geminate consonant in the underlying representation which cannot be present in the singular or singulative forms. Further, the underlying syllable structure may be different in the two forms (SG/PL).

When the rules summarized below are applied to the underlying representations, words can be successfully derived. In the case of nouns, inflected forms, which at first glance seem to behave in an arbitrary fashion, can be derived in a straightforward manner. Utilizing the same set of rules, several verb forms can also be successfully derived.

By utilizing syllable structure rules, it is no longer necessary to posit rules which will link or delink a consonant or vowel at crucial points. Instead, the syllable structure rules explain where these insertions and/or deletions will be and why they are there.

A summary of the syllable constraints, and rules are given below. First, the constraints and conventions.

(310) INITIAL CONSONANT SEQUENCE

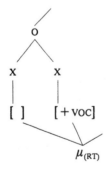

Shilluk Phonology

(311) INITIAL CONSONANT SEQUENCE CONSTRAINT

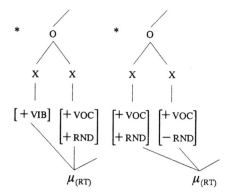

(312) INITIAL GEMINATE CONSONANT CONSTRAINT

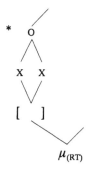

(313) GLIDE AND VOWEL CONSTRAINT

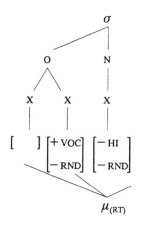

148   Shilluk Syllable Structure

(314) SYLLABLE HEAD CONSTRAINT (SHC)

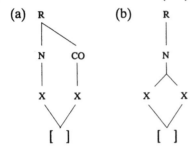

(315) BRANCHING CODA CONSTRAINT (BCC)

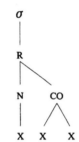

(316) PHONOLOGICAL WORD LEVEL CONSTRAINT (PWL)

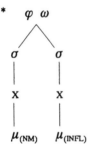

(317) MARKED VOWEL CODA CONSTRAINT (MVCC)

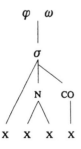

Shilluk Phonology

(318) VOCALIC ASSOCIATION CONSTRAINT (VAC)

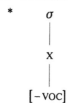

(319) VOCALIC DELINKING (VD)

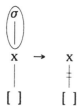

(320) SEGMENT DELINKING CONVENTION (SDC)

Rules:

(321) CODA SYLLABIFICATION (RIGHTMOST SELECTION) PRINCIPLE (CSP)

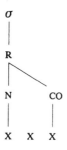

(322) DUAL SYLLABLE HEAD PRUNING RULE (DSHP)

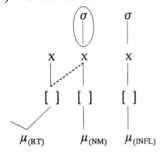

(323) MARKED VOWEL CODA DELINKING (MVCD)

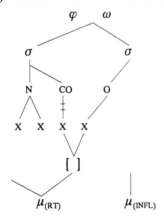

(324) (optional) PLURAL METATHESIS RULE (PMR)

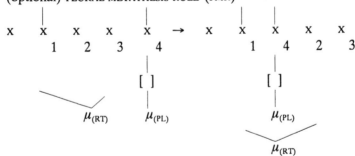

Shilluk Phonology

(325) SYLLABLE HEAD MOVEMENT (SHM)

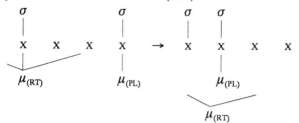

(326) NUCLEAR ADJUNCTION (NA)

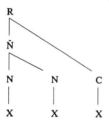

This results in a complex nucleus.

(327)

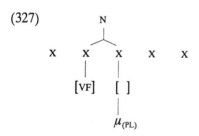

(328) ROOT VOWEL SPREADING RULE (RVSR)

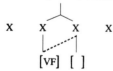

(329) ROOT-FINAL CONSONANT DELINKING RULE (RFCDR)

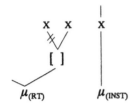

Abbreviations

BCC	(237)	BRANCHING CODA CONSTRAINT
CSP	(238)	CODA SYLLABIFICATION PRINCIPLE
DSHP	(256)	DUAL SYLLABLE HEAD PRUNING RULE
MVCC	(263)	MARKED VOWEL CODA CONSTRAINT
MVCD	(267)	MARKED VOWEL CODA DELETION
NA	(289)	NUCLEAR ADJUNCTION
PMR	(287)	PLURAL METATHESIS RULE
PWL	(255)	PHONOLOGICAL WORD LEVEL CONSTRAINT
RFCDR	(308)	ROOT-FINAL CONSONANT DELINKING RULE
RVSR	(291)	ROOT VOWEL SPREADING RULE
SDC	(239)	SEGMENT DELINKING CONVENTION
SHC	(234)	SYLLABLE HEAD CONSTRAINT
SHM	(288)	SYLLABLE HEAD MOVEMENT
VAC	(235)	VOCALIC ASSOCIATION CONSTRAINT
VD	(236)	VOWEL DELINKING

5
Lexical Levels of Derivation

This chapter deals with assigning tone and harmonic features to the stem and to the word. The task of assignment will introduce the various levels on which different affixes operate. As the rules are discussed, it will be shown how they operate at the various levels within the lexicon. Tone and its assignment and rules will be examined first. Then, under the harmony section, we will consider vowel, vowel-consonant and consonant harmony. Finally, there is a process of nasalization affecting the nouns which is triggered by the addition of certain inflections to singular nouns. At the end of the chapter is a listing of all the rules and the levels in which they apply.

5.1. Tone

In chapter 2, we saw that there are three underlying level tones in Shilluk. Then again, in chapter 3, we saw that tone is lexical. In chapter 4 tone was shown to have morphemic status in the verbs. In §4.8, we saw that the instrument forms of the verb have M-M tone while the benefactive consistently has M-H. Singular and plural nouns also have distinctive tones such that MH is only found in singular words while HM is only found with plural words. Thus, tone can be viewed as a morpheme.

It was not made clear, however, how tones are assigned to words. The problem of tone assignment will be discussed and several options presented. Once a satisfactory solution has been found, the discussion will turn to tone rules as they interact with the morphology. We will then see how these rules are ordered with regard to the levels within the lexicon.

Tone association. According to Goldsmith (1976) the segmental features and the tonal features are connected by association lines. These association lines are subject to the WELL-FORMEDNESS CONDITION. The WELL-FORMEDNESS CONDITION as it relates to tone and association conventions is presented in (330).

(330) WELL-FORMEDNESS CONDITION
  a. Association lines do not cross.
  b. All tone-bearing units (TBU) are associated to at least one tone.
  c. All tones are associated to at least one tone bearing unit.

The associations themselves are carried out by means of the ASSOCIATING CONVENTIONS (see van der Hulst and Smith 1985a:17).

(331) ASSOCIATING CONVENTIONS (AC)
  a. Mapping
     Insert association lines between one tone and one TBU—going from left-to right/right-to-left, starting with the left/rightmost tone and TBU
  b. Dumping
     Left over tones are associated to the nearest TBU to their right/left
  c. Spreading
     Left over TBU's are associated to the nearest tone to their left/right

Limitations have also been proposed for representations. The OBLIGATORY CONTOUR PRINCIPLE (OCP) was originally proposed by Leben (1973). It has undergone some modifications since its inception. The definition for the OCP which will be used in this paper comes from McCarthy (1986:208) and says "at the melodic level, adjacent identical elements are prohibited".

Using the guidelines set out above, I will try to associate the tonal morpheme tier to one-, two-, and three-syllable words in Shilluk. As has been previously discussed, the timing tier is the backbone of the autosegmental framework. All planes attach to this central point, and thus relate to each other.

Example (332) gives the underlying representation for the word álwē:dɔ́ 'crab' from chapter 3.

Shilluk Phonology 155

(332)

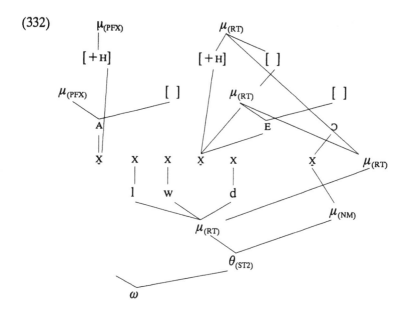

The ROOT is not a simple element. It is composed of a complex of morphemes and features; namely, the V and C tiers, [EX] and tone. This complex functions as a unit, even though the individual elements are capable of independent extraction. In addition to the root there is a complex of morphemes which composes the prefix and another set for the suffix. The root and the affixes combine to yield one member of a singular/plural or FORM A/FORM B stem pair. For a given member, the vocalic melody, [EX] and tone are invariant.

The representation shown in (332) is the more accurate way in which to demonstrate the interrelationships among the morpheme, root, stem, word, tone, [EX], vowel, consonant, etc. for one member of the pair, but it does not lend itself to easy interpretation when shown on two-dimensional paper. Since most of my discussion in this chapter is concerned with only one or two tiers at a time, it would add unnecessary complexity to an already intricate subject to include the required information in this appropriate and yet cumbersome representation. Therefore, I will take the liberty of substituting a simpler (if outmoded and inaccurate) representation type. This alternative representation involves the use of bracket notation. The same word *álwē:dɔ́* 'crab' will be shown in (333).

(333) [$_{WD}$a[$_{ST}$[$_{RT}$ lwe:d]$_{RT}$ɔ]$_{ST}$]$_{WD}$

156   Lexical Levels of Derivation

Tone will be associated directly to the vowel since the vowel is the tone-bearing unit for Shilluk.

This change in notation in no way represents a change to bracketing. The brackets and subscripts used will only be employed to indicate the morpheme boundaries in a simpler notation so that the particular topic under discussion can be highlighted.

The CVC configuration which is the basis of almost all Shilluk words will be termed the root. In its neutral or unmarked form (SG or COLL), the root is presumed to have a zero suffix. Thus, the surface form of the root and the stem will be identical. Further discussion of root and stem is found in the next section.

Tone assignment. Initially, let us assume that the tonal tier is associated to the x slot which is also associated to a syllable head and [+ voc] feature matrix. We may invoke the one-to-one mapping principle given in the ASSOCIATING CONVENTIONS.

(334) INITIAL TONE ASSOCIATION RULE (ITAR)

Associate the first tone with the first tone bearing unit.

Then, tones are mapped from left to right onto the tone-bearing units. It will be recalled that the M tone or [−H−L] is the underspecified tone, indicated by empty brackets ([ ]).

(335) $\begin{bmatrix} \text{H} [ ] \text{L} \\ \text{/adyeljwɔk/} \end{bmatrix} \rightarrow \begin{bmatrix} \text{H} [ ] \text{L} \\ | \\ \text{adyeljwɔk} \end{bmatrix} \rightarrow \begin{bmatrix} \text{H} [ ] \text{L} \\ | \; | \; | \\ \text{[adyeljwɔk]} \end{bmatrix}$ 'butterfly'
                                 ITAR   map

If there are more tone-bearing units than tones, then spreading (SP) could be invoked in accordance with the ASSOCIATING CONVENTIONS to associate the last tone onto the remaining tone-bearing units. This would appear to explain the tone patterns of words such as in (336).

(336) $\begin{bmatrix} \text{H L} \\ \text{/adṵːlɔ/} \end{bmatrix} \rightarrow \begin{bmatrix} \text{H L} \\ | \\ \text{adṵːlɔ} \end{bmatrix} \rightarrow \begin{bmatrix} \text{H L} \\ | \; | \\ \text{adṵːlɔ} \end{bmatrix} \rightarrow \begin{bmatrix} \text{H L} \\ | \; \diagdown \\ \text{[adṵːlɔ]} \end{bmatrix}$ 'circle'
                    ITAR   map   SP

Shilluk Phonology   157

While such steps will work for many words in the language, they will
certainly not begin to account for all the data. Consider the tone patterns
in the words of (337).

(337) áŋʉ́dɪ̱   'spitoon'
       ópâ:dɔ́   'broken pot'
       gâm:ɪ̱   'midwives'
       ácʉ̀ŋɔ̀   'black mound termite'
       ákô:ɖɔ́   'shrew'
       bʉ́dɔ̀   'long term illness'

In these words we see that there are several ways in which to combine
the tones. The device we have so far limits us in the options for combining
tones unless we mark all the exceptions in the lexicon. That approach is
not satisfactory. Let us look at a putative derivation in order to pinpoint
the problem.

(338) $\begin{bmatrix} H\ [\ ] \\ /aŋʉdi/ \end{bmatrix} \rightarrow \begin{bmatrix} H\ [\ ] \\ aŋʉdi \end{bmatrix} \rightarrow \begin{bmatrix} H\ [\ ] \\ aŋʉdi \end{bmatrix} \rightarrow \begin{bmatrix} H\ [\ ] \\ *[aŋʉdi] \end{bmatrix}$ 'spitoon'
                       ITAR   map   SP

The tone on *[áŋʉ́dɪ̱] is incorrect since the H tone should have been on
the root [ŋʉ́d] and then the M tone should associate with the suffix.
Perhaps, then, the tone should associate to the tone-bearing unit in the
root. Before proceeding further, then, it is necessary to define terms such
as root and stem.
     The cvc configuration which is the basis of almost all Shilluk words will
be termed the root. In its neutral or unmarked form (SG or COLL), the root
is presumed to have no suffix. Thus, in the surface form both root and the
stem will be co-extensive.

(339)
       $[_{ST}[_{RT}\quad]_{RT}]_{ST}$ = simple stem = $\mu_{(RT)}$
                                                       |
                                                       θ

When the form is a morphologically marked form such as the SGLT or PL,
then there is a number suffix (NM) which is outside the root but inside the
stem. The need for this distinction will become clearer as we proceed.

158   Lexical Levels of Derivation

(340)

$[_{ST} [_{RT} \quad]_{RT} \text{ NM}]_{ST}$ = complex stem $= \overset{|}{\mu}_{(RT)} \quad \overset{|}{\mu}_{(NM)}$

θ

We will assume that prefixes are outside the stem since the stem may have a distinct meaning in its own right. The addition of a prefix would add a new and often unpredictable dimension to that meaning.

(341)

$[_{WD} \text{ PFX } [_{ST}[_{RT} \quad]_{RT} \text{ NM}]_{ST}]_{WD}$ $= \overset{|}{\mu}_{(PFX)} \quad \overset{|}{\mu}_{(RT)} \quad \overset{|}{\mu}_{(NM)}$

θ

ω

Within this framework, it is possible to set up the tone association rule to assign the tone to the root. Once the tone is mapped onto the root, let us adopt a hypothesis that spreading may occur from left to right and right to left.

(342) ROOT ASSOCIATION RULE (RAR)

Associate tones with the first vocalic x slot associated to the syllable head of root.[16]

(343) $\begin{bmatrix} \text{H} [\ ] \\ [o[[pa{:}d]o]] \end{bmatrix} \underset{\text{RAR}}{\rightarrow} \begin{bmatrix} \text{H} [\ ] \\ \overset{V}{opa{:}do} \end{bmatrix} \underset{\text{SP}}{\rightarrow} \begin{bmatrix} \text{H} [\ ] \\ ópa{:}dɔ \end{bmatrix}$ 'broken pot'

(344) $\begin{bmatrix} \text{HL} \\ [a[[ko{:}d]o]] \end{bmatrix} \underset{\text{RAR}}{\rightarrow} \begin{bmatrix} \text{HL} \\ \overset{V}{ako{:}do} \end{bmatrix} \underset{\text{SP}}{\rightarrow} \begin{bmatrix} \text{HL} \\ ako{:}dɔ \end{bmatrix}$ 'shrew'

---

[16]In (343), it should be noted that the underspecified tone is allocated in the same way as H or L tone. For the moment, spreading is assumed to account for association of tone to the stem suffix since that is the process for H and L tones. However, underspecified features are not actually allowed to spread. At the end of the derivation, all units without an assigned H or L tone will be assigned M tone [−H−L].

Shilluk Phonology

If, however, we apply these steps to a word such as the one considered in (336), we are again in trouble.

$$(345) \quad \begin{bmatrix} \text{HL} \\ [a[[dul]ɔ]] \end{bmatrix} \xrightarrow[\text{RAR}]{} \begin{bmatrix} \text{HL} \\ \diagdown\!\diagup \\ adulɔ \end{bmatrix} \xrightarrow[\text{SP}]{} \begin{bmatrix} \text{HL} \\ \diagup\!\diagdown\!\diagdown \\ *[adulɔ] \end{bmatrix} \text{'circle'}$$

The HL sequence has associated to the root, when only the L tone should have done this. Clearly this hypothesis was wrong. The problem is to find an analysis which can account for all the possible combinations of tones shown in (337).

Assignment by levels. In the solution offered, we will recognize levels in the derivation. We will look at each step to see how the tone pattern for the word is brought about. We begin with simple noun stems, and then move on to the complex stem form.

Simple stem words. Tone comes to be associated to the root in the lexicon. In the case of neutral forms (SG/COLL), the tone is associated to the root vowel by the ASSOCIATING CONVENTIONS. Roots in Shilluk have a CVC structure and simple stems have no suffix. Therefore, these words are monosyllabic.

$$(346) \quad \begin{bmatrix} \text{H} \\ [\text{ST} [\text{RT} \text{ bak}] \text{RT}] \text{ST} \end{bmatrix} \xrightarrow[\text{RAR}]{} \begin{bmatrix} \text{H} \\ | \\ [\text{bak}] \end{bmatrix} \text{'garden'}$$

$$(347) \quad \begin{bmatrix} [\ ] \\ [[byer]] \end{bmatrix} \xrightarrow[\text{RAR}]{} \begin{bmatrix} [\ ] \\ | \\ [byer] \end{bmatrix} \text{'roots'}$$

Complex stem words. For the morphologically marked (SGLT/PL) words, there appear to be two cases which must be dealt with. In the first case, seventy percent of the words have a number marker (NM) which is toneless. If the NM has no specified tone, the root tone spreads. In the event that the root tone is assigned a sequence of two tones, the second tone is the one that spreads onto the syllable head of the number marker.

160   Lexical Levels of Derivation

The NM is within the stem. Since no other suffixes are allowed in the stem itself, it will be assumed that the second syllable head within the brackets is stipulated to be the NM. It will be recalled that the NM is in the stem but outside the root.

(348) $[_{ST}[_{RT}]_{RT} \text{NM}]_{ST}$

Thus, the tone association would be as in (349).

(349) $\begin{bmatrix} \text{H} \\ [[\text{dɔːr}]\text{ɔ}] \end{bmatrix} \rightarrow \begin{bmatrix} \text{H} \\ | \\ [[\text{dɔːr}]\text{ɔ}] \end{bmatrix} \rightarrow \begin{bmatrix} \text{H} \\ \diagup \\ [[\text{dɔːr}]\text{ɔ}] \end{bmatrix}$ 'axe'
$\qquad\qquad\qquad$ RAR $\qquad\qquad$ SP

(350) $\begin{bmatrix} [\ ]\text{L} \\ [[\text{bu̠g}]\text{ɔ}] \end{bmatrix} \rightarrow \begin{bmatrix} [\ ]\text{L} \\ \diagup \\ [[\text{bu̠g}]\text{ɔ}] \end{bmatrix} \rightarrow \begin{bmatrix} [\ ]\text{L} \\ \diagup \\ [[\text{bu̠g}]\text{ɔ}] \end{bmatrix}$ 'cow with dead calf'
$\qquad\qquad\qquad$ RAR $\qquad\qquad$ SP

The tone is initially associated to the root. Since the NM suffix is toneless, the last tone on the root spreads onto it.

In the remaining thirty percent of cases, the NM suffix has a preassociated tone. This tone would be assigned in the lexicon and can be any of the three level tones (H M L). Since there is already a tone assigned to the suffix, no spreading occurs from the root.

(351) $\begin{bmatrix} \text{H L} \\ | \\ [[\text{bu̠d}]\text{ɔ}] \end{bmatrix} \rightarrow \begin{bmatrix} \text{H L} \\ | \ | \\ [[\text{bu̠d}]\text{ɔ}] \end{bmatrix}$ 'long-term illness'
$\qquad\qquad\qquad$ RAR

Stem external tones. At this point, we will begin to examine the prefix tones which are considered to be outside of the stem.

(352) $[_{WD}[_{ST}[_{RT}]_{RT}]_{ST}]_{WD}$

In the previous analysis of (343) and (344), an hypothesis was put forward to the effect that the root tone spreads to the left to fill in the prefix tone. Even apart from the patent inadequacy of that hypothesis to account for forms such as (336), statistically, this analysis is highly questionable since the prefix tone and the initial root tones are identical only

Shilluk Phonology   161

about forty-five percent of the time. In the remaining fifty-five percent of cases, the prefix tone is different from the root tone. Given this information, it seems reasonable to say that prefix tone is tagged as a morpheme which is preassociated to the appropriate x slot of the prefix.

(353) $\begin{bmatrix} \text{H} \quad \text{L} \\ | \\ [a[[cuŋ]ɔ]] \end{bmatrix}$ → $\begin{bmatrix} \text{H} \quad \text{L} \\ | \quad | \\ [a[cuŋɔ]] \end{bmatrix}$ → $\begin{bmatrix} \text{H} \quad \text{L} \\ | \quad \backslash \\ [acuŋɔ] \end{bmatrix}$ 'black mound termite'
                                      RAR   SP

(354) $\begin{bmatrix} \text{H} \quad \text{HL} \\ | \\ [a[[koːɖ]ɔ]] \end{bmatrix}$ → $\begin{bmatrix} \text{H} \quad \text{HL} \\ | \quad \bigvee \\ [a[koːɖɔ]] \end{bmatrix}$ → $\begin{bmatrix} \text{H} \quad \text{HL} \\ | \quad \bigwedge \\ [akoːɖɔ] \end{bmatrix}$ 'shrew'
                                      RAR   SP

It will be recalled that the OBLIGATORY CONTOUR PRINCIPLE requires a unitary representation of adjacent identical elements. However, in this case, we are dealing with two morphemes, namely, the prefix and the stem. These two morphemes function on different planes and are thus not subject to the constraints of the OCP. We will see a similar situation with regard to the [EX] harmonic tier.

Tone on inflections. The word, in Shilluk, is a whole unit with its own integral meaning. However, one may add inflections such as the referential determiner *-ání* or possessive determiners. When these inflections are added to the word, some radical changes occur such as stem-final consonant gemination in SGLT words as well as vowel shortening or lengthening. These changes have been discussed at length in chapter 4. For our purposes in this chapter, these inflected forms will occur outside the word.

(355) $[_{WD}[_{WD} \text{PFX}[_{ST}[_{RT} \quad]_{RT}]\text{NM}]_{ST}]_{WD} \text{INFL}]_{WD}$

The tone assigned to *-ání* is H. In compliance with the OBLIGATORY CONTOUR PRINCIPLE, only one H is assigned to the unit, and spreading is allowed from left to right.

162   Lexical Levels of Derivation

(356)
$$\left[\begin{array}{c} \text{H L}\qquad\text{H} \\ |\qquad\quad| \\ [[\text{a}[\text{cʊ̰ŋ}]\text{ɔ̰}][\text{ani}]] \end{array}\right] \rightarrow \left[\begin{array}{c} \text{H L}\qquad\text{H} \\ |\;\;|\qquad| \\ [\text{a}[\text{cʊ̰ŋ:}][\text{ani}]] \end{array}\right] \rightarrow \left[\begin{array}{c} \text{H L}\;\;\text{H} \\ |\;\;|\;\;/\!: \\ [\text{acʊ̰ŋ:ani}] \end{array}\right]$$
                    RAR   SP

In this derivation, the H is preassociated to the PFX and the L is assigned
to the root. Yet another H is assigned to the morpheme -*ani*. This H
assignment is preferred since the H can spread and preassociated tones
cannot spread. We know from chapter 4 that the -ɔ is delinked because of
the DUAL SYLLABLE HEAD PRUNING RULE. The root-final consonant spreads
into the slot previously linked to the vowel. Since the syllable head has lost
its vocalic content, it can no longer receive a tone assignment. The only
spreading that can occur in this word is within the -*ání* unit. Thus, we end
up with the correct form [ácʊ̰ŋ:ání] 'this black mound termite'.

We turn now to the possession markers. Their tone is assigned by the
number category of the noun to which they are attached. The possessive
tone assignment is made on the basis of the *semantic* singular or plural
category rather than the *morphological* singular or plural distinction. In
order to clarify this point, the (±PL) is marked at the *word* level rather
than at the morpheme level.

The tone on the possession marker (PS) of a semantically singular noun
will be M while the tone of the PS for plural nouns will be H. We will
assume, then, that the PS have no inherent tone, but receive the tone
assignment from the number category of the noun they possess.

(357) POSSESSIVE TONE ASSIGNMENT (PTA)

$$\begin{array}{cc} \quad[\ ] & \qquad\qquad[+\text{H}] \\ \quad| & \qquad\qquad\quad| \\ \omega_{(-\text{PL})}\quad\mu_{(\text{PS})} & \qquad\omega_{(+\text{PL})}\quad\mu_{(\text{PS})} \end{array}$$

For the sake of simplicity in the examples, the bracketing will not include
all possible levels for monosyllabic words. A root which has no suffix and
no prefix is identical to the word. Therefore, in the examples, only the
noun word bracketing is shown. (The reader will recall that the brackets
only express a simplified representation of the morphological information.)

Shilluk Phonology 163

(358)
$$\left[\begin{array}{c} \text{L} \\ [_{WD}[_{-PL} \text{ bul}]_{-PL} \text{ [e]}_{PS}]_{WD} \end{array}\right] \underset{\text{PTA}}{\rightarrow} \left[\begin{array}{c} \text{L[ ]} \\ [[\text{bul}]\text{e}] \end{array}\right] \underset{\text{RAR}}{\rightarrow} \left[\begin{array}{c} \text{L [ ]} \\ [[\text{bul}]\text{e}] \end{array}\right] \text{'his drum'}$$

(359)
$$\left[\begin{array}{c} \text{L} \\ [_{WD}[_{PL} \text{ d\d{a}t:}]_{PL} \text{ [e]}_{PS}]_{WD} \end{array}\right] \underset{\text{PTA}}{\rightarrow} \left[\begin{array}{c} \text{L\ \ H} \\ [[\text{d\d{a}t:}][\text{e}]] \end{array}\right] \underset{\text{RAR}}{\rightarrow} \left[\begin{array}{c} \text{L\ H} \\ [\text{d\d{a}t:e}] \end{array}\right] \text{'its hooves'}$$

Compound words. Finally, we come to tones assigned to words which have two stems. It will be recalled that genitives (especially SGLT or PL words) have an *-i* possessive marker between two nouns. In the case of a compound word, this is not the case. The full forms of both words are present. True compounds are composed of separate words with no intervening marker. These compounds may be noun + noun or noun + verb. The extent of possibilities has not yet been fully investigated.

The process for assigning tone is essentially the same as with simple words in that both stems have tones assigned. Consider the word *a\d{t}ur\d{o}wic* 'house of the king'. I do not know the meaning of *\d{t}ur\d{o}*, but *wic* means 'head'.

(360)
$$\left[\begin{array}{ccc} \text{L}\ \ \ \ \text{L} & & \text{HL} \\ [_{WD}\ \text{a}[_{ST}[_{RT}\ \text{\d{t}ur}]_{RT}\ \text{\d{o}}]_{ST}[_{ST\ D\ wic}]_{ST}]_{WD} \end{array}\right] \underset{\text{RAR}}{\rightarrow} \left[\begin{array}{ccc} \text{L}\ \ \text{L} & & \text{HL} \\ [\text{a}[[\text{\d{t}ur}]\d{o}][\text{wic}]] \end{array}\right] \underset{\text{SP}}{\rightarrow} \left[\begin{array}{ccc} \text{L L} & & \text{HL} \\ [\text{a\d{t}ur\d{o}wic}] \end{array}\right]$$

As shown in (360), the prefix tone is preassigned while the two root tones receive their tone by the ASSOCIATING CONVENTIONS. The ROOT ASSOCIATION RULE links the root tones to the first vocalic x slot in the root. Then, spreading may occur, in this case, to the NM suffix of the first root. This process gives the correct output [à\d{t}ùr\d{ɔ}wîc] 'house of the king'.

Morphotonemics. Initially, the various rules for tone will be discussed. Once these rules have been identified, we will see how they apply within the level-ordering of the lexicon.

In chapter 4, a rule was given whereby the vowel specifying number was delinked. According to Leben (1978), when a vowel is deleted, the tone remains as a floating tone. A floating tone is a result of a deleted vowel. The tone may be reassociated to the tone-bearing unit that conditioned the delinking or loss of syllabicity (Clements and Ford 1979). The effects

164   Lexical Levels of Derivation

of the floating tone are usually seen in the following tone. The convention given by Leben (1980:45) states that "a rule mapping a suprasegmental tone onto a segment already specified for a tonal feature does not replace this feature but instead adds another tone feature in sequence".

Tone delinking with complex stems. Shilluk does not appear to have floating tones. The evidence suggests that when the vowel suffix is delinked, the tone is delinked as well as in (361) and (362).

(361)

	+PS	+ání	
dɔ́:rɔ́	dɔ́:rē	dɔ́:rání	'axe'
bã:ɲɔ̄	bã̱ɲ:ē	bã̱ɲ:ání	'grasshopper'
bã̱:lɔ̄	bã̱l:ē	bã̱l:ání	'scar'
tṳk:ḭ	———	tṳk:ání	'rocks of mud'

(362)

byɛ̱̀:lɔ́	byɛ̱l:ē	byɛ̱l:ání	'stalk of millet'
gám:ɪ̱̄	gám:é	gám:ání	'midwives'
bṳ́dɔ̰̀	bṳ́n:ē	bṳ́n:ání	'zucchini'

In these examples, we see words which receive part of their tone structure by spreading (361) and others which have preassigned tones (362). Let us consider the underlying structure of each case.

(363)
$$
\begin{bmatrix} [\ ]_L \\ [[ba:l]ɔ] \end{bmatrix} \xrightarrow[\text{RAR}]{} \begin{bmatrix} [\ ]_L \\ [ba:lɔ] \end{bmatrix} \xrightarrow[\text{SP}]{} \begin{bmatrix} [\ ]_L \\ [ba:lɔ] \end{bmatrix}
$$

(364)
$$
\begin{bmatrix} H\,L \\ [[bṳd]ɔ] \end{bmatrix} \xrightarrow[\text{RAR}]{} \begin{bmatrix} H\ L \\ [bṳdɔ] \end{bmatrix}
$$

When an inflectional morpheme is added to these words, we see from the examples that the final stem tone does not appear. We know from chapter 4 that NM suffixes are delinked when inflectional suffixes are added. The syllabicity is lost triggering the stem-final consonant to spread to the x slot to its right (see DUAL SYLLABLE HEAD PRUNING RULE §4.3). Since only vowels bear tone in Shilluk, if a vowel is delinked from the timing tier, its tone will receive no phonetic realization.

Shilluk Phonology

(365) TONE DELETION RULE (TDR)

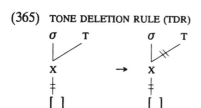

Consider the full derivation.

(366a)   (366b)

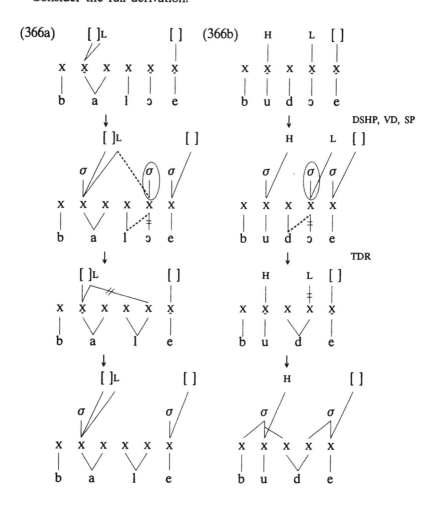

So, we see from these examples that when the syllable head is lost, the tone is also delinked. This principle applies to tones which spread from the root and to tones which are preassigned.

Interestingly, when the vowel in the root is reduced, as in (366a), if we continue the derivation, the tone is not shortened. Both M and L occur on the short stem vowel.

(367)

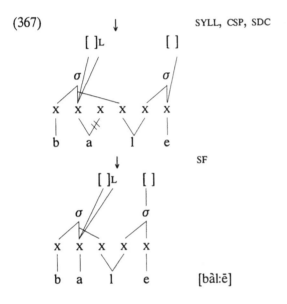

Before drawing any conclusions about this interesting tonal behavior, it is important to look at words which are morphologically simple.

Tone delinking with simple stems. We will now turn our attention to words with simple stems which means that there is no number marker. Consider the following data.

(368)
	+PS	+ání	
bâŋ	bá:ŋē	bá:ŋání	'servant'
bāt	bā:dē	bā:nání	'arm'
kwàr	kwā:rē	kwā:rání	'grandchild'
byĕc	byè:jē	byè:ɲání	'cow with horns straight out'

(369)
| ámăl | ámàl:é | ámàl:ání | 'camels' |
| cyḛw | cyḛw:é | cyḛw:ání | 'porcupines' |

Shilluk Phonology 167

The words included here are singular (368) and collective (369). From the examples, we see that the second tone of the sequence of root tones fails to appear in the inflected form. This pattern differs dramatically from the complex stems examined earlier where the contour tone is evident on the root vowel in the inflected form.

There are two ways in which to handle the retention and deletion of tone sequences. It is possible to posit a rule such that if two distinct tones are associated to a stem, the $T_{(n-1)}$ is delinked in the presence of an inflection. In this way, the generalization of losing the second stem tone would be captured.

(370) T_1 T_2 T
        θ $\mu_{(INFL)}$ (T_2 is distinct from T_1)

In order to adequately handle the data, this analysis would probably involve positing a copy rule instead of a spreading rule in order to account for the tone on the number suffix. However, if this analysis were followed, we would miss a greater generalization in Shilluk. Later, we will see that there is a nasalization rule which applies to a complex stem, but not to a simple stem (§5.3). The tone rule expressed below reflects this same distinction between the complex and simple stems. Thus, this second analysis seems to present a more systematic approach.

A rule more clearly describes the simplification of a root contour tone with a simple stem. Then, a comparative derivation of the two types has to be set up.

(371) TONE SIMPLIFICATION RULE for unmarked nouns (TSR)

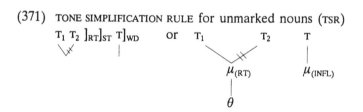

The TONE SIMPLIFICATION RULE says that when a simple noun stem with a sequence of two tones is inflected, the second tone of the sequence is delinked. The derivations of both SG and SGLT words follow.

168　　　　　　　　　　　　　　　　　Lexical Levels of Derivation

(372)

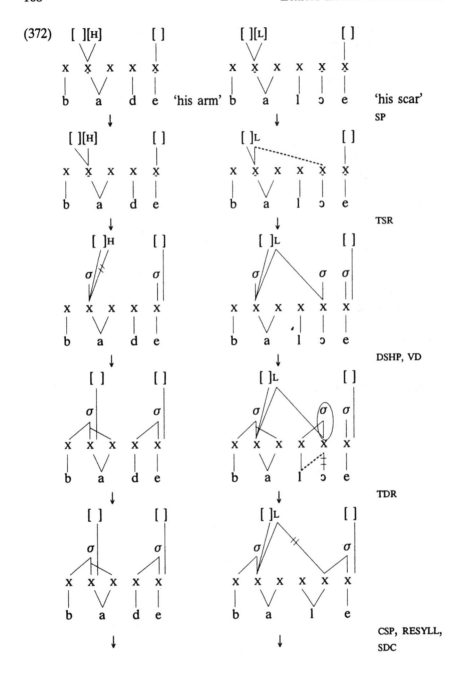

Shilluk Phonology

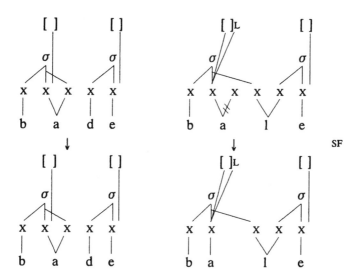

Within the framework of lexical phonology, there are at least two modules, the lexical and the postlexical. Within the lexical module, there are presumed to be various levels or strata. The number of levels and the content of each level seem to be language specific. The levels in the lexicon contain both morphological and phonological information. The phonological information has access to the morphological information present at that level. With Shilluk, the lexical rules are assumed to apply in blocks such that rules which relate to the root apply first, then those relating to the stem and finally to the word. All morphological information is retained throughout the derivation until the planes conflate just before the postlexical level. Following Cole (1987), the BRACKET ERASURE CONVENTION does not apply until the end of the lexical level.

If we apply this concept to the derivation just shown for Shilluk nouns, we see that at this point there are two morphological levels. In the first of these two levels, the TONE ASSIGNMENT is made to the root. The morphology differentiates simple stems from complex stems. The TONE SIMPLIFICATION RULE applies to simple stems (i.e., neutral nouns), and so is enacted first. Spreading also occurs to the head of the complex stem in *ba:ɔ+e* 'his scar'.

Secondly, the DUAL SYLLABLE HEAD PRUNING RULE rule is implemented to eliminate the dual syllable heads. In the process, the vocalic content of the number marker is delinked. The TONE DELETION RULE then delinks the tone since there is no longer any vocalic content in that segment.

Were the DUAL SYLLABLE HEAD PRUNING RULE rule to occur before the TONE ASSIGNMENT and TONE SIMPLIFICATION RULE, then the syllable head of the number suffix would have been pruned. Both the morphologically marked and unmarked forms would then be identical, from a syllable head point of view. The result of that would be that the TSR could apply equally to both. Application of the TSR to the previously complex stems would result in incorrect forms.

Tone delinking with derived plurals. It will be recalled from chapter 4 that many plural words undergo what may be generally termed the I-INCORPORATION PROCESS (IIP). This process involves both SYLLABLE HEAD MOVEMENT and a change in syllable structure. With regard to the levels in the lexicon, it seems that IIP is implemented at a later level. The ordering becomes clear when we examine the tone rules. Let us first look at the data, and then continue the analysis.

(373) PL   PL+PS   PL+*ání*
       bâ:ɲ   *báɲ:é*   *báɲ:ání*   'mosquitos'
       bâ:c   ———   *bác:ání*   'outer layers of plants'
       gwɔ̂:k   *gwɔ́k:é*   *gwɔ́k:ání*   'dogs'
       kwɔ̂:m   *kwɔ̀m:é*   *kwɔ̀m:ání*   'seats for chiefs'

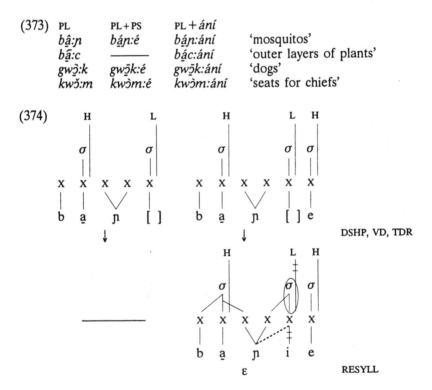

Shilluk Phonology

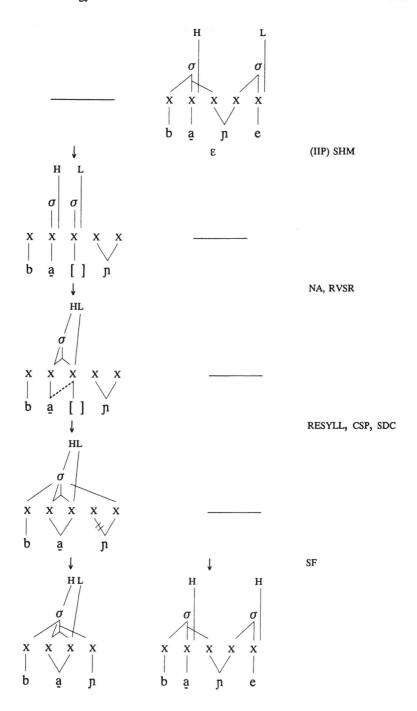

172   Lexical Levels of Derivation

This derivation reveals two important points. First, this ordering allows the derivation to proceed without any new rules. Only the tone rules previously set up are needed to obtain the correct surface form.

Secondly, the I-INCORPORATION PROCESS applies after the DUAL SYLLABLE HEAD PRUNING RULE and TONE DELETION RULE at level two. The plural marker moves into the root by the process demonstrated in chapter 4. If the number suffix is preassociated, then that tone will also move into the root and a tone sequence will surface. The result, in this case, is a HL sequence on the root vowel. Evidence of this movement of tone was given in §4.6. The frequency of complex tones on plural words would easily be accounted for by this analysis. Underlyingly, the tones are level, but the derivation process results in a contour tone on the surface. The level ordering in the lexicon as we now understand it looks like this:

> Root level: TA, PTA, TSR, SP
> Stem level: DSHP, TDR, SYLL, CSR, SDC
> Word level: IIP: SHM, NA, RESYLL including CSR and SDC

In conclusion, then, we have seen evidence to show that there are at least three levels in the lexicon in Shilluk. At the root level, TONE ASSIGNMENT is made to the root. If a noun has a simple stem, then it may be subject to the TONE SIMPLIFICATION RULE, if the structural conditions are met. If it is a complex stem, then SPREADING may occur.

On the stem level, an inflected complex stem undergoes the DUAL SYLLABLE HEAD PRUNING RULE to conform with the PHONOLOGICAL WORD LEVEL CONSTRAINT which disallows two syllable heads from occurring contiguously. The TONE DELETION RULE will come into effect when an x slot loses its [+voc] content. The tone will be delinked from that x slot since the conditions of syllable headedness and vocalic content are no longer present. Finally, the SYLLABIFICATION process and the CODA SIMPLIFICATION RULE will apply.

At the word level, the I-INCORPORATION PROCESSES of SYLLABLE HEAD MOVEMENT and NUCLEAR ADJUNCTION apply. It will be recalled that this process only occurs with certain specified lexical items. The application of the rules is dependent on the morphological information to identify the root and stem. Therefore, this process must be included within the lexical level. RESYLL will take place, including another application of CODA SIMPLIFICATION RULE and SEGMENT DELINKING CONVENTION since syllabification is perseverative. Once the word is properly syllabified, it can leave the lexical level and proceed to the postlexical module. It is assumed that the planes are conflated at the end of the final lexical level (cf. Cole 1987).

Shilluk Phonology   173

Having established level-ordering in the lexicon, and how the tone assignment fits into those levels, let us turn to another plane, that of harmony.

5.2. Harmony systems

Within Shilluk, there are three harmony systems at work. First we will consider the vowel harmony. Secondly, we will examine the relationship between the root vowel and the final consonant. Finally, there is evidence of some consonant harmony. We will present the data for each of these systems and show how the data may be analyzed along the same lines as the tonal system.

Vowel harmony. As stated in chapter 2, there are two sets of vowels [±EX]. The term advanced tongue root [ATR] has frequently been used as the distinctive feature for these vowels. However, Lindau (1974, 1979) has argued persuasively for a more accurate term; namely, expanded pharynx [EX]. The two sets of Shilluk vowels are listed below followed by some examples.

(375)   [−EX]   [+EX]
         i   o   i̠   u̠
         e   ɔ   e̠   ɔ̠
            a   a̠

(376)   +PS   +ání
       àdè:rɔ̀   àdè:rē   àdè:ráni̠   'donkey'
       ádɔ̠:gɔ̠   ádɔ̠:gē   àdɔ̠:ɲáni̠   'cow's first milk'

(377) byél   byél:é   byél:áni̠   'millet (PL)'
       pì:nɔ̀   pìn:ē   pìn:áni̠   'wasp'
       pì̠:nɔ̠   pìn:ē   pìn:áni̠   'cheek'
       dí̠twɔ̠l dí̠twɔ̠lē   dí̠twɔ̠láni̠   'black and white bull'
       ɲáɲâŋ   ———   ɲáɲá:ɲáni̠   'type of lizard'
       ògwàl   ògwà:lē   ògwà:láni̠   'frog'
       ògwɔ̠l   ògwɔ̠:lē   ògwɔ̠:láni̠   'sacred ibis'

An investigation of the data shows that there are some consistent points regarding the [EX] feature. First, we notice that all prefixes are [−EX]. The root, however, may be either [+EX] or [−EX]. Looking further, we see that the number suffix agrees with the root with regard to its [EX] value as in

174   Lexical Levels of Derivation

(376). The possessive suffix (PS), however, is always [−EX]. It is not possible for the vowel harmony to influence the PS suffix, nor, in fact, the -ání suffix 'this'.

Following the bracketing set up in §5.1, we have the formula in (378).

(378) [$_{WD}$[$_{WD}$ PFX[$_{ST}$[$_{RT}$]$_{RT}$ NM]$_{ST}$]$_{WD}$ INFL]$_{WD}$

If we assign an [EX] feature to the root, that feature will spread to the NM suffix in the stem. Unlike the tones, the NM suffix *always* agrees with the root [EX] feature. Thus, we can formally express the [EX] association rule as in (379).

(379) ROOT ASSOCIATION RULE for [EX]

       Associate [EX] feature to the root.

We understand, of course, that [EX] is a feature which normally associates with a vowel. We can see this process in the monosyllabic word shown in (380).

(380) $\begin{bmatrix} [-EX] \\ [[byEl:]] \end{bmatrix} \xrightarrow[RAR]{} \begin{bmatrix} [-EX] \\ | \\ [byEl:] \end{bmatrix}$ 'millet'

In this representation, an upper case letter is used to indicate the VOWEL HEIGHT. Before the addition of the [EX] feature, it is unspecified for that feature. The uppercase letter, then, signifies that that vowel is unspecified for [EX]. As in previous examples of this type, the phonetic symbol is also used as a shorthand for a set of distinctive features.

In the case of a complex stem, the ROOT ASSOCIATION RULE is applied and spreading (SP) is allowed by the ASSOCIATING CONVENTIONS.

(381) $\begin{bmatrix} [-EX] \\ [[pɪ:n]ɔ] \end{bmatrix} \xrightarrow[RAR]{} \begin{bmatrix} [-EX] \\ | \\ [pɪ:nɔ] \end{bmatrix} \xrightarrow[SP]{} \begin{bmatrix} [-EX] \\ \diagdown \\ [pɪ:nɔ] \end{bmatrix}$ 'wasp'

(382) $\begin{bmatrix} [+EX] \\ [[pɪ:n]ɔ] \end{bmatrix} \xrightarrow[RAR]{} \begin{bmatrix} [+EX] \\ | \\ [pɪ:nɔ] \end{bmatrix} \xrightarrow[SP]{} \begin{bmatrix} [+EX] \\ \diagdown \\ [pɪ:nɔ] \end{bmatrix}$ 'cheek'

Shilluk Phonology   175

As was the case with the tones, spreading is only allowed within the stem. The only possibility, then, is left to right spreading.

At the word level, we find a prefix. As was stated earlier, the prefix in Shilluk always has a [−EX] value. There are two ways to deal with this fact. First, one can simply preassign a [−EX] value to the prefix. This approach had to be adopted for the tones. The consistency (100%) with which the [−EX] feature occurs on a prefix would indicate that it receives its [EX] assignment quite independently of the root. The derivation would look like (383).

(383)
$$
\begin{bmatrix} [-\text{EX}][+\text{EX}] \\ | \\ [\text{A}[[\text{dɔːg}]\text{ɔ}]] \end{bmatrix} \rightarrow_{\text{RAR}} \begin{bmatrix} [-\text{EX}][+\text{EX}] \\ | \quad | \\ [\text{A} \quad [\text{dɔːgɔ}]] \end{bmatrix} \rightarrow_{\text{SP}} \begin{bmatrix} [-\text{EX}][+\text{EX}] \\ | \quad \diagup | \\ [\text{Adɔːgɔ}] \end{bmatrix} \text{ 'cow's first milk'}
$$

The root would receive an assignment which eventually spreads to the stem suffix. However, all of this procedure rapidly becomes cumbersome and redundant. So, we will look at a second approach to the analysis.

When there is a binary feature system, it is useful to combine the theories of markedness and underspecification (Archangeli 1984). Within underspecification theory, only distinctiveness is required underlyingly. The redundant features are supplied by rule. Thus, the lexical representations of the language are streamlined.

In applying underspecification to vowel harmony in Shilluk, we may say that the value [+EX] is selected. The [−EX] value is not stated, but is left as the unspecified value. It is filled in later by a complement rule.

(384) COMPLEMENT RULE FOR [EX] (CR-[EX])

[ ] → [−EX]

By the COMPLEMENT RULE, any vowel underspecified with respect to [EX] will receive a [−EX] value at the end of the derivation.

The end result of this process is that only root vowels with a [+EX] value are marked as such in the underlying representation. The [−EX] value is filled in by rule. It seems clear, then, that the [+EX] value is the marked value. This hypothesis agrees with findings by van der Hulst (personal communication) that the [+ATR] is the more marked value across languages. Utilizing underspecification, we may derive words in the following way.

176   Lexical Levels of Derivation

(385) $\begin{bmatrix} [+\text{EX}] \\ \\ [_A[[d\text{ɔ:g}]\text{ɔ}]] \end{bmatrix} \underset{\text{RAR}}{\rightarrow} \begin{bmatrix} [+\text{EX}] \\ | \\ [_A[[d\text{ɔ̇:g}]\text{ɔ}]] \end{bmatrix} \underset{\text{SP}}{\rightarrow} \begin{bmatrix} [+\text{EX}] \\ \\ [_A[d\text{ɔ:gɔ}]] \end{bmatrix} \underset{\text{CR}}{\rightarrow} \begin{bmatrix} [-\text{EX}][+\text{EX}] \\ | \quad \wedge \\ [_A \ d\text{ɔ:gɔ}] \end{bmatrix}$

(386) $\begin{bmatrix} \\ \\ [_A[[d\text{E:r}]\text{ɔ}]] \end{bmatrix} \underset{\text{CR}}{\rightarrow} \begin{bmatrix} [-\text{EX}][-\text{EX}][-\text{EX}] \\ | \quad | \quad / \\ [_A \quad d\text{E:r} \quad \text{ɔ}] \end{bmatrix}$

In the examples above, the [−EX] is left unspecified. Root assignment and spreading apply as before. However, at some later point, the [−EX] feature is assigned by the COMPLEMENT RULE. It is assumed that a feature specification assigned in this way does not spread, but that any vowel which does not have an assignment for [EX] will receive a minus value.

Along a similar line, it was noted in the examples (376) and (377) that all inflections are [−EX]. (It will be recalled that NM suffixes have a special status in the stem, and thus are not included in the present discussion of inflections.) Again, we could specify them in the representation, but that is highly redundant. Instead, they can be left underspecified, and the value will be filled in by the COMPLEMENT RULE.

Before completing the derivation, one more rule is needed. The [EX] feature normally attaches to a vowel. If the syllable head is pruned, then the vocalic tier element is disassociated along with any dependent autosegments, specifically, [EX].

(387) [EX] DELETION RULE ([EX]DR)

σ

|

x

‡ __ [EX]

[ ]

Shilluk Phonology 177

(388)

$$\begin{bmatrix} [+\text{EX}] \\ [[_A[d\text{ɔ:g}]\text{ɔ}][\text{E}]] \end{bmatrix} \xrightarrow[\text{RAR}]{} \begin{bmatrix} [+\text{EX}] \\ [[_A[d\text{ɔ:g}]\text{ɔ}][\text{E}]] \end{bmatrix} \xrightarrow[\text{SP}]{} \begin{bmatrix} [+\text{EX}] \\ [[_A d\text{ɔ:g}\text{ɔ}][\text{E}]] \end{bmatrix}$$

$$\xrightarrow[\text{DSHP, VD, [EX]DR}]{} \begin{bmatrix} [+\text{EX}] \\ [_A d\text{ɔ:g:}[\text{E}]] \end{bmatrix} \xrightarrow[\text{CR}]{} \begin{bmatrix} [-\text{EX}][+\text{EX}][-\text{EX}] \\ [_A \quad d\text{ɔŋ:} \quad \text{E}] \end{bmatrix}$$

In this derivation, the [+EX] feature is associated to the root. After spreading occurs, the DUAL SYLLABLE HEAD PRUNING RULE prunes the syllable head on the number suffix. When the vocalic content is delinked, the [EX] feature is no longer allowed to surface. The COMPLEMENT RULE fills in the [−EX] values for the prefix and inflection. The nasalization of the final plosive is explained in §5.3.

Now let us look at a slightly more elaborate example *aṭurɔwic* 'house of the king'. This word has a prefix, a complex stem, and a simple stem.

(389)

$$\begin{bmatrix} [+\text{EX}] \\ [_A[[ṭor]\text{ɔ}][\text{WIC}]] \end{bmatrix} \xrightarrow[\text{RAR}]{} \begin{bmatrix} [+\text{EX}] \\ [_A[[ṭor]\text{ɔ}][\text{WIC}]] \end{bmatrix} \xrightarrow[\text{SP}]{}$$

$$\begin{bmatrix} [+\text{EX}] \\ [_A[ṭor\text{ɔ}][\text{WIC}]] \end{bmatrix} \xrightarrow[\text{CR}]{} \begin{bmatrix} [-\text{EX}] [+\text{EX}] [-\text{EX}] \\ [_A \quad ṭor\text{ɔ} \quad \text{WIC}] \end{bmatrix}$$

In the derivation, we see that the first stem has a [+EX] feature. The ROOT ASSOCIATION RULE and spreading apply within the stem. The COMPLEMENT RULE fills in the [−EX] value for the prefix and the simple stem [wic].

In conclusion, we find that the vowel harmony system can be easily analyzed by much the same means as the tonal system. The analysis of the vowel harmony, however, is more straightforward than for the tone since it is possible to mark only the [+EX] feature on the stem. All instances of [−EX] are filled in by a COMPLEMENT RULE. The [EX] association takes place at the root level and spreading at the stem level. If the [−EX] CR applies postlexically, then there is no chance for harmony to start erroneously at the left end of the word instead of at the root. This analysis would lessen

178   Lexical Levels of Derivation

the already heavy memory load and presents a streamlined and accurate
account of the data.

Stem vowel and final consonant alternation. We come now to an interesting sideline within Shilluk phonology. This particular aspect of the
phonology has been mentioned in the past by Kohnen and others, but no
attempt has been made to offer any explanation for it. The discussion
offered here is not intended to resolve the questions, but is included with
the expectation that it may prompt other suggestions on ways to approach
the issue. The topic at hand is the interaction between the vowel and
consonant tiers within the root of Shilluk words. Consider the following
sets of nonalternating (390) and alternating (391) words.

(390)   Word (1)   Word (2)

    gɔ̄:l   *gɔ̂:l*   'wild dog/s'
    àcwíl   *àcwî:l*   'brown cow/s'
    béṭ   *biṭ:i*   'fish spear/s'
    bāt   *ba̠:t*   'arm/s'
    dút   *dũ̠:t*   'loin cloth/s'
    gwar   *gwa:r*   'to snatch (FORM A/FORM B)'
    ḍur   *ḍur*   'to push'
    maṭ   *ma:ṭ*   'to drink'

(391)   Word (1)   Word (2)

    lwɔ̂l   *lɔ̠t*   'gourd/s'
    pāl   *pâ̠t*   'spoon/s'
    kâ:l   *ka̠:t*   'cattle camp/s'
    bul   *but*   'to broil (FORM A/FORM B)'
    ma:r   *ma̠:t*   'to love'
    gwi:r   *gwi̠:t*   'to prepare'
    cwɔl   *cwɔt:i*   'to call'
    tyel   *tyeṭ:i*   'to pull'
    bel   *biṭ:i̠*   'to taste'
    ṭal   *ta:t*   'to cook'
    byel   *byeṭ:i*   'to carry'
    kɔl   *kɔ:t*   'to herd away'
    col   *cut*   'to pay'

Focusing on the root final consonants of these words, we see in the first
set (390) that the final consonant of each pair of words is the same. These
words represent the regular pattern of the language.

In the second set of words (391), we find that between the two forms
there is an alternation of the root final consonant between the liquids and

Shilluk Phonology 179

the voiced alveolar plosive /d/. The alternation seems to be directly related to the [EX] value of the root vowel. The liquids are found after [−EX] vowels while the alveolar plosive occurs after the [+EX] vowels.

These liquid/plosive alternations are irregular and should not be looked upon as representing a fully productive process. They have become lexicalized and could be looked upon as historic relics.

Looking at the process itself, we see that the primary alternation is between a root final [l] and [t]. (The rules given in chapter 2 account for a syllable final /d/ becoming [t]. See §2.4.) The second alternation is between [r] and [t]. The conditioning factor for this alternation seems to be the feature [±EX]] on the preceding root vowel.

Let us suppose that consonants as well as vowels are specified as having an [EX] feature. Unlike the vowels, however, any of which can have either [±EX], the consonants would be specified as [−EX] except for the /d/ which would be [+EX] and the alternating /L/ and /R/ which would have no specification for [EX]. Thus, the regular /l r/ (non-alternates) would be preassociated with [−EX] as in (392).

(392)   x
          |
      [+COR]
          |
      [−EX]

The non-alternating /d/ would be as in (393).

(393)   x
          |
      [+COR]
          |
      [+EX]

The alternating consonants, then, would have the [+COR] feature specified, but no [EX] specified. The [EX] value is spread or perhaps copied from the [EX] feature associated with the root vowel (394).

(394)

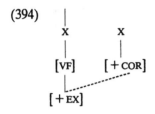

Phonetically, then, the [+COR, +EX] is realized as [d] and the [+COR, −EX] could be [l] or [r] depending on the other features in the matrix.

Of course, all of the suggestions here are highly speculative. First of all, [EX] has never been proposed as a consonant feature. Besides, it seems somewhat extreme to propose such a major addition to the distinctive feature matrix to account for these two alternating consonants, especially as they have non-alternating counterparts. In addition to these problems, [−EX] has been suggested as the underspecified value. Yet, in this particular approach, all consonants other than /d/ and the two alternating ones would have to have a [−EX] specification in order not to receive the [EX] value from the root vowel. That would seem to leave open the possibility of a ternary system of [+EX], [−EX] and [ ]. Unfortunately, I have no solution to this dilemma and so am forced to leave it as a residual problem which needs further consideration.

Consonant harmony. Consonant harmony is limited to the root. Furthermore, it only concerns alveolar or dental stops.

(395) Dental   Alveolar

  àḍúṯ 'stinger' dút 'loin cloth'
  búḍɔ̰ 'zucchini' búdɔ̰ 'long illness'
  ṯi̱n 'small' ti̱n 'today'
  wâṯ 'bull' wât 'son'
  ṯɔ́l 'rope' túl 'forehead'
  cyà̱ṯɔ̰ 'a walk' cyá̱:dɔ̰ 'likeness'

In actual fact, we are dealing with a constraint on consonants occurring together. Within a root, the [+COR, +OCC] consonant may be specified for [αAPI] as in (396).

Shilluk Phonology

(396)

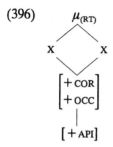

Again, the minus value will be the underspecified one so that we have the COMPLEMENT RULE for [API] in (397).

(397) [ ] → [−API]

Thus, we have the following derivation.

(398) $\begin{bmatrix} [+\text{API}] \\ [\text{TIN}] \end{bmatrix}$ 'small' $\begin{bmatrix} [\ ] \\ [\text{TIN}] \end{bmatrix}$ 'today'

↓ ↓

$\begin{bmatrix} [+\text{API}] \\ [\text{TIN}] \end{bmatrix}$ $\begin{bmatrix} [-\text{API}] \\ [\text{TIN}] \end{bmatrix}$

↓ ε

[ṭiṇ] [tin] SF

It is not possible for the [API] to spread onto the inflection as can be seen from (399).

(399) SG   SG + ání

búḍɔ̀   búṇ:ání   'zucchini'
wâṭ   wá:ṇání   'bull'
ṭɔ́l   ṭɔ́:lání   'rope'

We see that the -ání is unaffected by the apical feature and remains an alveolar stop even when all other consonants in the root are dental. A derivation is shown in (400).

182   Lexical Levels of Derivation

$$(400) \quad \begin{bmatrix} [+\text{API}] \\ \mid \\ [[[\text{waːT}]][\text{aNi}]] \end{bmatrix} \underset{\text{RAR}}{\rightarrow} \begin{bmatrix} [+\text{API}] \\ \mid \\ [[[\text{waːT}]][\text{aNi}]] \end{bmatrix} \underset{\text{CR[API]}}{\rightarrow} \begin{bmatrix} [+\text{API}][-\text{API}] \\ \mid \quad / \\ [[\text{waːT}][\text{aNi}]] \end{bmatrix}$$

$$\underset{\text{RDNA}}{\rightarrow} \begin{bmatrix} [+\text{API}][-\text{API}] \\ \mid \quad / \\ [\text{waːNani}] \end{bmatrix} \quad \text{'this bull'}$$

In (400), the [+API] feature attaches to the [+COR] plosive at the root level and spreading occurs in the stem level. However, in accordance with the regular pattern in the lexical level for Shilluk, the [+API] feature cannot spread beyond the stem into the word. Thus, the underspecified alveolar consonant in the inflection (-*ání*) correctly surfaces as the alveolar nasal. The [+API] feature cannot affect it. The nasalization process is a regular feature of singular words and is covered in §5.3.

5.3. Inflected singular nouns

In this section, I deal with a process of nasalization which occurs with singular words (used in the more general sense). The first half of this section is concerned with the addition of the referential determiner inflection. If a singular noun root ends in a plosive, the addition of -*ání* will result in the oral plosive becoming a nasal.

A similar process of nasalization occurs with the possessive marker. This process will be covered in the second half of the section. The difference between the PS and the -*ání* is that only the SGLT nouns undergo the nasalization with the PS.

Referential determiner inflection. When the referential determiner -*ání* 'this' is added to a singular word with a plosive as the root final consonant, the plosive undergoes nasalization. This nasalization process occurs with singular words, but never with plural or collective forms as seen in (401) and (402).

Shilluk Phonology

(401) SG   SG+ání   PL+ání
       gwɔ̂k   gwɔ̂:ŋání   gwɔ̂k:ání   'dog'
       gwɔ̄k   gwɔ̄:ŋání   gwɔ̄k:ání   'work'
       yép   yé:mání   yép:ání   'tail'
       àkɔ̂c   àkɔ̂:ɲání   àkɔ̂c:ání   'pair of shorts'
       àcwā̱t   àcwā̱:ṉání   àcwā̱t:ání   'guinea fowl'

(402) SGLT   SGLT+ání   PL+ání
       lwē:dɔ̄   lwén:ání   lwét:ání   'finger'
       pwɔ̀:ḍɔ́   pwɔ̀ṉ:ání   pwɔ̄ṯ:ání   'field'
       álwē:dɔ̄   álwén:ání   álwét:ání   'crab'
       búḍɔ̀   bún:ání   būṯ:ání   'corgettes'
       ápwɔ̀:jɔ̀   ápwɔ̀ɲ:ání   ápwɔ́c:ání   'rabbit'
       cɔ̀:gɔ̀   cɔ̀ŋ:ání   cūr:ání   'bone'

As we can see from these data, the plosives in stem final position mutate to a nasal at the same point of articulation. The gemination in the second set of words is derived by rules already set up. So, how do we account for this nasal assimilation?

Since the nasalization process only occurs with singular words, it is necessary for that morphological information to be available. Otherwise, the ordering of this step does not seem to be crucial. The NASALIZATION RULE would state that if the referential determiner inflection is added to a semantically singular noun, a [+NAS] feature is attached to the root-final consonant.

The NASALIZATION RULE in (403) says that if that root-final consonant is a [+OCC], then the [+NAS] feature is added to the feature complex of that consonant. The phonetic result is that all occlusives become nasals. The difference between the SG referential determiner (RD) -ání and the plural -ání is the addition of the [+NAS] morpheme which indicates singularity.

(403) REFERENTIAL DETERMINER NASAL ATTACHMENT (RDNA)

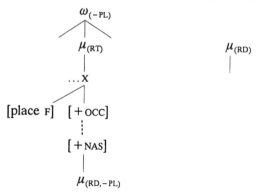

184   Lexical Levels of Derivation

Thus, when the referential determiner is added to a semantically singular noun which also has a root-final consonant which is [+occ], the morpheme [+NAS] attaches to that root-final consonant.

The plural -*ání* has no extra element. This is clear from the fact that it may simply be added to the plural noun as an inflection.

Possessive inflection. When the possessive inflection is added to a singular noun, the result depends on whether the noun is SGLT or SG. This distinction is somewhat reminiscent of the tone rules which were set up at the beginning of this chapter.

(404) SG   SG + PS
      gwô̰k   *gwó̰:gē*   '(his) dog'
      gwɔ̄k   *gwɔ̄:gē*   '(his) work'
      yɛ́p   *yɛ́:bē*   '(his) tail'
      àkɔ̰c   *àkɔ̰:jē*   '(his) pair of shorts'
      àcwa̰ɬ   *àcwa̰:ɬē*   '(his) guinea fowl'

(405) SGLT   SGLT + PS
      lwē:dɔ́   *lwén:ē*   '(his) finger'
      pwɔ̰:dɔ́   *pwɔ̰n:ē*   '(his) field'
      álwē:dɔ́   *álwén:ē*   '(his) crab'
      bṵ́dɔ̰   *bṵ́n:ē*   '(his) corgettes'
      ápwɔ̰:jɔ̰   *ápwɔ̰n:ē*   '(his) rabbit'
      cɔ̰:gɔ̰   *cɔ̰n:ē*   '(his) bone'

In (404) we notice that the SG + PS forms have no nasalization process. However, in the SGLT forms (405) there is a nasal process at work. The simplest way to handle this distinction is to say that POSSESSIVE NASAL ATTACHMENT only occurs with singular nouns with complex stems. This addition of the nasal feature would have to be ordered early on before the DUAL SYLLABLE HEAD PRUNING RULE rule so that the presence of the SGLT suffix -ɔ + PS could trigger the association of the [+NAS] morpheme indicating singularity.

Shilluk Phonology

(406) POSSESSIVE NASAL ATTACHMENT (PNA)

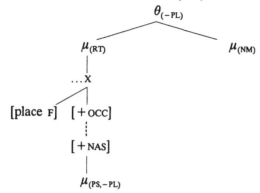

The PNA rule says that semantically singular words with complex stems (i.e., SGLT words) which also have a [+occ] root-final consonant, will receive a [+NAS] morpheme attachment when a possessive morpheme is added to the word.

5.4. Summary of levels and rules

Let us summarize and review the various rules which have been posited in this chapter within the levels in which they apply. Of necessity, some rules have been developed in other chapters.

At the beginning of the derivation, the ROOT ASSIGNMENTS for tone, [EX], [API], and POSSESSIVE TONE ASSIGNMENT are made.

(407) ROOT ASSOCIATION RULE (RAR) (generalized)

Associate the feature with the first feature bearing unit in the root.

The OBLIGATORY CONTOUR PRINCIPLE applies within the limit of the root to each of these features. Thus, spreading may apply by the ASSOCIATING CONVENTIONS from the root to the stem.

We saw evidence that some tones are assigned according to the grammatical category. Specifically, the tone on the possessive marker is assigned according to the morphological singular or plural category of the noun to which it is attached. The related rule is shown in (408).

(408) POSSESSIVE TONE ASSIGNMENT (PTA)

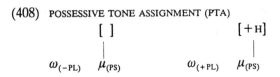

The TONE SIMPLIFICATION RULE also applies here.

(409) TONE SIMPLIFICATION RULE for unmarked nouns (TSR)

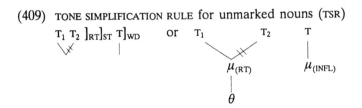

While the information regarding singular noun is still available, the [NAS] morphemes indicating singularity must be included.

(410) REFERENTIAL DETERMINER NASAL ATTACHMENT (RDNA)

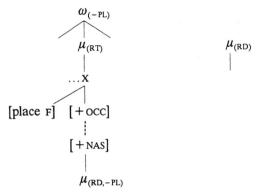

Shilluk Phonology

(411) POSSESSIVE NASAL ATTACHMENT (PNA)

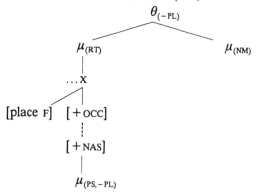

At the stem level, the DUAL SYLLABLE HEAD PRUNING RULE (§4.3), CODA SYLLABIFICATION PRINCIPLE and SEGMENT DELINKING CONVENTION (§4.1) apply. The CSP and SDC will reapply at all levels in order to correctly resyllabify the string during the derivation. There are also several rules which deal with the deletion or delinking of features. These are listed below.

(412) TONE DELETION RULE (TDR)

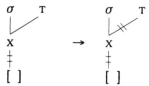

(413) [EX] DELETION RULE ([EX]DR)

At the word level, the I-INCORPORATION PROCESS applies. The rules included here are SYLLABLE HEAD MOVEMENT, NUCLEAR ADJUNCTION as well as the ROOT VOWEL SPREADING RULE (§4.6).

Finally, the COMPLEMENT RULES are used to fill in the minus values in the appropriate matrices.

188 Lexical Levels of Derivation

(414) COMPLEMENT RULE FOR [EX] (CR-[EX])

$$[\ ] \rightarrow [-\text{EX}]$$

(415) COMPLEMENT RULE FOR [API] (CR[API])

$$[\ ] \rightarrow [-\text{API}]$$

Abbreviations

([EX]DR)	(387)	[EX] DELETION RULE
(PNA)	(406)	POSSESSIVE NASAL ATTACHMENT
(PTA)	(357)	POSSESSIVE TONE ASSIGNMENT
(RAR)	(342)	ROOT ASSOCIATION RULE
(RDNA)	(403)	REFERENTIAL DETERMINER NASAL ATTACHMENT
(TSR)	(371)	TONE SIMPLIFICATION RULE
(TDR)	(365)	TONE DELETION RULE

6
Summary and Conclusions

6.1. Advantages of generative phonology

The nonlinear generative approach combined with lexical phonology and underspecification theory seem to offer the simplest and most economical analysis of the language. Distinctive features are assumed to have their own tier or plane.

Lexical phonology allows rules to be ordered in such a way so as to include morphological information. There are three blocks of rules which apply within the Shilluk lexicon. Rules which do not need morphological information in their structural description and apply consistently are found in the postlexical module.

Underspecification theory enables us to simplify the amount of LEARNED information since only DISTINCTIVENESS is specified. All other values are filled in by default rules.

These three theories have combined to supply an adequate account of Shilluk. There is only one major point at which the Shilluk data departs from the expected. The point in question does not contest any of these phonological theories, but does question a general assumption made about underlying representations.

6.2. Independent underlying representations

One of the most interesting aspects of Shilluk phonology is found in the underlying representations of the nouns and transitive verbs. When two forms of a word, such as singular and plural, utilize variants of a single morpheme, then it should be possible to give a unique representation to

189

190   Summary and Conclusions

that morpheme. Rules are used to convert a single underlying representation into its surface alternates (Schane 1973:74–5). Thus, the singular and plural forms should be derived from a common source, except words whose forms are suppletive.

It is at this point that Shilluk seems to part company with linguistic expectation. It is not possible to derive Shilluk singulars and plurals or transitive verb forms from a single underlying representation. In chapter 3, numerous points of variability (§3.2) are discussed. There is unpredictable variation in 1) the initial root consonant (cw or cy alternates with c), 2) the root-final consonant (/l/ or /r/ sometimes alternates with /d/), and 3) the root vowel. With regard to the root vowel, it is impossible to predict 1) the feature [EX], 2) the vowel height (E~I, O~ɔ, E~A) or 3) the tone. Further discussion in chapter 4 shows that structurally too there may be a difference between singular and plural at the level of the underlying representation. The plural forms have root-final geminate consonants whereas the singular words have only a single root-final consonant.

There is a distinction drawn in Shilluk between words which are related and those which are suppletive. [gìn] and [jámːɪ̰] 'thing/s' are suppletive while [waːl] and [wa̰ːt] 'to boil' are related. The deciding factors in determining the relationship seem to rest on the words having the same initial consonant and a predictable (within certain limits) final consonant in the root. In neither case, are both of the forms derivable from a common or unique underlying representation. Thus, two forms for each morpheme must be learned by the language learner.

6.3. Implications for language learning

This claim for independent underlying representations has obvious implications for linguistics, particularly in the area of child language acquisition. Since all children are assumed to learn language at the same rate, there would seem to be similar processes at work for all language learners.[17] If Shilluk children must memorize the singular and plural of nouns and the FORM A and FORM B of every transitive verb without the benefit of a common underlying representation and derivational rules, then it would imply that children learning other languages *may* be memorizing

---

[17]Observation of Shilluk children raised in a multilingual situation indicate that their language development is within the expected norms. The one child I have been able to observe personally is being raised in London, England in a tri-lingual situation. At 18 months of age, she has begun using one word utterances in Shilluk. This behavior seems to be well within normal developmental limits.

Shilluk Phonology 191

more than had been thought. If so, the memory load and the capacity for learning this amount of material is far greater than has previously been assumed. Although one case is insufficient evidence to disprove a theory of the presence of single underlying forms, it is enough to raise a question about them.

6.4. Syllable structure

Syllable structure is another area of study to which Shilluk data provides some valuable insights. It is suggested in this study that there are two syllable structures available for Shilluk roots. These two structures account for words whose root vowel is either INVARIABLY SHORT, INVARIABLY LONG or ALTERNATINGLY SHORT AND LONG as was seen in chapter 4.

Syllable structure rules account for the alternation of vowel length and the gemination of some root-final consonants. One of the most interesting aspects of Shilluk syllable structure is found in the I-INCORPORATION PROCESS described in §4.6. The -i suffix is, on occasion, moved into the root vowel of the word. The result is a change of syllable structure in that form to an INVARIABLY LONG vowel. However, the other forms of that word typically have ALTERNATINGLY SHORT AND LONG vowels in the root. Through this process, we may deduce that a concatenative language is becoming a non-concatenative one.

Syllable structure rules apply perseveratively in Shilluk. Rules are sensitive to syllable structure such that whenever a structure is altered, the result must comply with syllable structure constraints. If an element cannot be syllabified, then that element cannot appear on the surface. Thus, syllable structure accounts simply and economically for variations of forms that would otherwise require numerous ad hoc rules.

6.5. Composition of Shilluk words

In Shilluk words, the basic element is the root. The root is normally composed of the pattern CVC. The stem would be made up of the root plus a number suffix. Any prefix attached to the stem is considered to be on a separate level. This structure is a phonological word. Other suffixes may be added as inflections to a word. Most phonological rules may only apply within the stem. The principle exception to that statement is syllable structure. Syllable structure rules apply perseveratively at all levels of derivation.

6.6. Features and feature assignments

The assignment of tone to the word is discussed in chapter 5. It was found that tone is assigned to the root and the WELL-FORMEDNESS CONDITIONS *may* apply as far as the stem. However, prefixes and inflectional suffixes have their own tone which are regarded as underived, i.e., preassociated.

Similarly, the [EX] feature is assigned to the root and spreads by the WELL-FORMEDNESS CONDITIONS to the stem. All prefixes and inflectional suffixes receive a [−EX] assignment.

In chapter 2, it is shown that there are three level tones in Shilluk. The M tone cannot be accounted for by means of assimilation, dissimilation, polarization, upstep, or downstep. Furthermore, all possible combinations of these three are found in sequences of tones (with the exception of LM). It is assumed, then, that the M tone is a distinctive level tone, but may be analyzed as the unmarked or underspecified tone. H means 'go up one step' and L means 'go down one step' (following Hyman 1986).

6.7. The lexicon

Within the lexicon, there are three levels or blocks of rules. Each level refers to a morphological level, i.e., root, stem, or word. The rules for each level are listed below.

Co-occurrence Condition and Constraints

(416) INITIAL CONSONANT SEQUENCE (ICS)

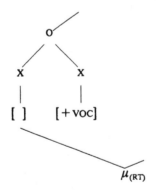

Shilluk Phonology

(417) INITIAL CONSONANT SEQUENCE CONSTRAINT (ICSC)

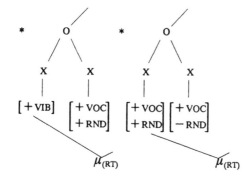

(418) GLIDE AND VOWEL CONSTRAINT (GVC)

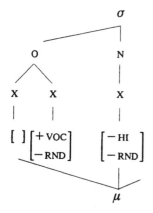

(419) INITIAL GEMINATE CONSONANT SEQUENCE CONSTRAINT (IGCSC)

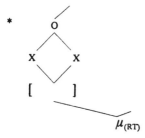

(420) TONE ASSOCIATION

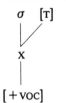

(421) SYLLABLE TEMPLATES

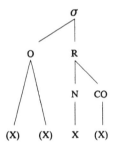

(422)

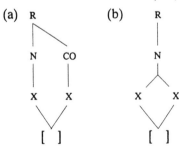

(423) SYLLABLE HEAD CONSTRAINT (SHC)

Shilluk Phonology

(424) VOCALIC ASSOCIATION CONSTRAINT (VAC)

(425) VOCALIC DELINKING (VD)

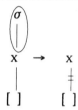

(426) BRANCHING CODA CONSTRAINT (BCC)

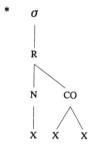

(427) SEGMENT DELINKING CONVENTION (SDC)

(428) PHONOLOGICAL WORD LEVEL CONSTRAINT (PWL)

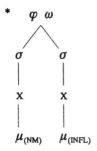

(429) MARKED VOWEL CODA CONSTRAINT (MVCC)

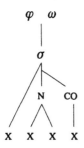

(430) ROOT ASSOCIATION RULE (RAR) (Generalized)

Associate the feature with the first feature bearing unit in the root.

Root level:

(431) POSSESSIVE TONE ASSIGNMENT (PTA)

(432) TONE SIMPLIFICATION RULE FOR UNMARKED NOUNS (TSR)

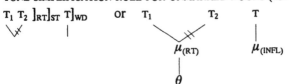

Shilluk Phonology

(433) REFERENTIAL DETERMINER NASAL ATTACHMENT (RDNA)

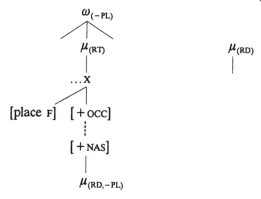

(434) POSSESSIVE NASAL ATTACHMENT (PNA)

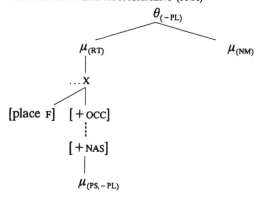

Stem level:

(435) CODA SYLLABIFICATION (RIGHTMOST SELECTION) PRINCIPLE (CSP)

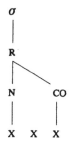

(436) DUAL SYLLABLE HEAD PRUNING RULE (DSHP)

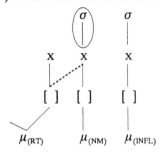

(437) MARKED VOWEL CODA DELINKING (MVCD)

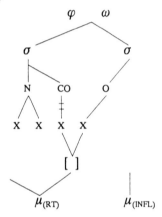

(438) TONE DELETION RULE (TDR)

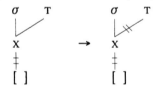

(439) [EX] DELETION RULE ([EX]DR)

Shilluk Phonology

Word level:

(440) (optional) PLURAL METATHESIS RULE (PMR)

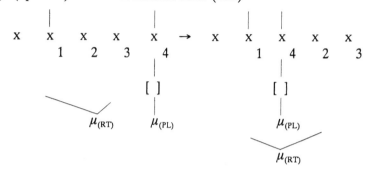

(441) SYLLABLE HEAD MOVEMENT (SHM)

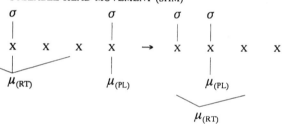

(442) NUCLEAR ADJUNCTION (NA)

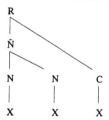

This results in a complex nucleus.

(443)

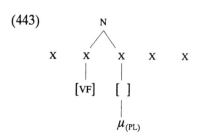

(444) ROOT VOWEL SPREADING RULE (RVSR)

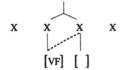

(445) ROOT-FINAL CONSONANT DELINKING RULE (RFCDR)

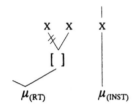

COMPLEMENT RULES apply as late as possible. They are listed below.

(446) COMPLEMENT RULE FOR [EX] (CR-[EX])

[ ] → [−EX]

(447) COMPLEMENT RULE FOR [API]

[ ] → [−API]

6.8. Postlexical level

After the lexical level, the postlexical rules are applied. Within the postlexical level, a new feature is introduced as a phonetic feature, namely, [tense]. This feature is explained in chapter 2. At present, the feature [TNS] is the result of an underlying structure, a geminate consonant. It may be, however, that in the future, this feature will become a distinctive feature in its own right. The feature [TNS] accounts for the fortis quality of the [+SON] consonants and the devoicing and aspiration of the [−SON] consonants.

Shilluk Phonology

(448) TENSING RULE (TR)

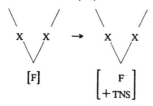

(449) PHONETIC SHORTENING RULE (PSR)

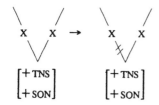

(450) SYLLABLE-FINAL DEVOICING (SFD)

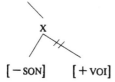

(451) TENSE-VOICING RULE (TVR)

$$[+\text{VOI}]$$
$$\updownarrow$$
$$X$$
$$|$$
$$\begin{bmatrix} +\text{TNS} \\ -\text{SON} \end{bmatrix}$$

(452) INTERVOCALIC ASPIRATION RULE (IAR)

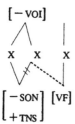

(453) DIPHTHONG HIGH SPREADING RULE (DHSR)

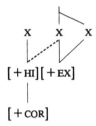

(454) OFF-GLIDE HIGH SPREADING RULE (OHSR)

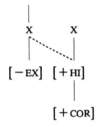

6.9. Further research

At the beginning of chapter 3, a synopsis of some main aspects of the syntax is given. There are many areas within the syntax which need further investigation. I will mention a few specific possibilities.

1) The verbal system of Shilluk would provide a very fertile area for research. The FORM A/FORM B system needs considerable study. Additionally, it should be noted that with auxiliary verbs, the ALTERNATINGLY SHORT AND LONG and INVARIABLY SHORT verbs use one while the INVARIABLY LONG words use FORM A/FORM B.
2) Topicalization and focalization as it relates to the surface word order.
3) The use of grammatical tone, particularly as it relates to the verbs. My research has concentrated primarly on tone in nouns.
4) Child language acquisition is a needed area of research.

Previous works on Shilluk have concentrated on providing a description of the language. Several orthographies for the Shilluk language have been developed on the basis of these studies. However, for most Shilluks, the results have been unsatisfactory.

Shilluk Phonology 203

In an attempt to develop a more acceptable orthography for the Shilluk language, it became necessary to discover a system that would explain the apparent inconsistencies of the language. One of the most significant insights resulting from this paper, from an orthographic point of view, is the inclusion of root-final geminate consonants.

I have begun work on this area of orthography already. It is hoped that the orthography to be proposed on the basis of the facts presented will represent more closely the perception that Shilluk people have of their language. Their response to that orthography will ultimately decide the accuracy of the conclusions presented here. As of 1991, the response of the Shilluk community to the orthography based on the analysis presented here has been enthusiastically positive. It is generally agreed that the new way of writing is very easy to read. Many have read with no instruction. Those with no previous knowledge of how to read Shilluk, but who read English or Arabic, can learn to read with the new system within one month.

As would be expected, however, the spelling has proven more of a challenge. A few have mastered it well. Most find they need much more practice. The challenge now is to teach non-literates to deal with the many interactions of syntax with their phonology.

References

Anderson, Stephen R. 1978. Tone features. In Victoria Fromkin (ed.), Tone: A linguistic survey, 133–76. New York: Academic Press.

Anonymous. 1935. Dholuo grammar. Nairobi: English Press Ltd. (Author—a member of St. Joseph's Society, Mill Hill, London).

Archangeli, Diana. 1984. Underspecification in Yawelmani phonology and morphology. Ph.D. dissertation, MIT, Cambridge, Mass.

Barahmen, M., S. Helsztyński and J. Kryanowski, eds. 1971. Studies in language and literature in honour of Margaret Schlauch. New York: Russell and Russell.

Belletti, A., L. Brandi, and L. Rizzi, eds. 1981. Theory of markedness in generative grammar. Proceedings of the GLOW Conference, 1979. Pisa: Scuola Normale Superiore di Pisa.

Boger, Koen, Harry van der Hulst, and Maarten Mous, eds. 1986. The phonological representation of suprasegmentals. Dordrecht: Foris.

Booij, Geert and Jerzy Rubach. 1987. Postcyclic versus postlexical rules in lexical phonology. Linguistic Inquiry 18:1–44.

Chomsky, Noam and Morris Halle. 1968. The sound pattern of English. New York: Harper and Row.

Clements, George N. 1985. The geometry of phonological features. In Colin J. Ewen and John M. Anderson (eds.), Phonology yearbook 2, 223–50. Cambridge: Cambridge University Press.

—— and Kevin C. Ford. 1979. Kikuyu tone shift and its synchronic consequences. Linguistic Inquiry 10:179–210.

—— and ——. 1981 On the phonological status of downstep in Kikuyu. In Didier L. Goyvaerts (ed.), Phonology in the 1980s, 309–58. Ghent, Belgium: E. Story-Scientia.

References

—— and John Goldsmith, eds. 1984. Autosegmental studies in Bantu tone. Dordrecht: Foris.

—— and Samuel J. Keyser. 1983. CV phonology. Cambridge, Massachusetts: MIT Press.

—— and Engin Sezer. 1982. Vowel and consonant disharmony in Turkish. In Harry van der Hulst and Norvil Smith (eds.), Structure of phonological representations 2, 213–56. Dordrecht: Foris.

Coates, Heather. 1985. Otuho phonology and orthography. In Mary Ruth Wise and Richard Watson (eds.), Occasional papers in the study of Sudanese languages 4:86–118. Juba, Sudan: Summer Institute of Linguistics and the Institute for Regional Languages.

Cole, Jennifer S. 1987. Planar phonology and morphology. Ph.D. dissertation, MIT, Cambridge, Massachusetts.

Crystal, David. 1985. A dictionary of linguistics and phonetics. Oxford: Basil Blackwell Ltd.

Dimmendaal, Gerrett. 1983. The Turkana language. African Languages and Linguistics 2. Dordrecht: Foris.

Ewen, Colin J. and John M. Anderson, eds. 1985. Phonology yearbook 2. Cambridge: Cambridge University Press.

Fishman, Joshua A., ed. 1986. The Fergusonian impact 1: From phonology to society. Berlin: Mouton de Gruyter.

Fromkin, Victoria A., ed. 1978. Tone: A linguistic survey. New York: Academic Press.

Goldsmith, John A. 1979. Autosegmental phonology. New York: Garland Press.

Goyvaerts, Didier L., ed. 1981. Phonology in the 1980s. Ghent, Belgium: E. Story-Scientia.

Haraguchi, Shosuke. 1977. The tone pattern of Japanese: An autosegmental theory of tonology. Tokyo: Hinode Printing Co.

——. 1987. On generalization in segmental phonology. In XIV International Congress of Linguists (Comité International Permanent des Linguistes), 10–15 August, 1987. Berlin.

Hayward, Richard J. 1986. The high central vowel in Amharic: New approaches to an old problem. In Joshua A. Fishman (ed.), The Fergusonian impact 1: From phonology to society. Berlin: Mouton de Gruyter.

Heasty, J. A. 1937. English-Shilluk, Shilluk-English dictionary. Doleib Hill, Sudan: The American Mission. (Reprinted 1974).

Hermans, Ben. 1985. The relation between aspiration and preaspiration in Icelandic. In Harry van der Hulst and Norvil Smith (eds.), Advances in nonlinear phonology, 237–66. Dordrecht: Foris.

Shilluk Phonology 207

Hock, Hans H. 1986. Compensatory lengthening: In defense of the concept 'mora'. Folia Linguistica 20.3–4.

Hyman, Larry. 1979. A reanalysis of tonal downstep. Journal of African Languages and Linguistics 1:9–29.

————. 1985a. A theory of phonological weight. Dordrecht: Foris.

————. 1985b. Word domains and downstep in Bamileke-Dschang. In Colin J. Ewen and John M. Anderson (eds.), Phonology yearbook 2, 47–84. Cambridge: Cambridge University Press.

————. 1986. The representation of multiple tone heights. In Koen Bogers, Harry van der Hulst, and Maarten Mous (eds.), Phonological representation of suprasegmentals, 109–52. Dordrecht: Foris.

Jacobson, Leon. 1980. Voice quality harmony in western Nilotic languages. In Robert M. Vago (ed.), Issues in vowel harmony. Proceedings of the Cuny Linguistics Conference on Vowel Harmony, 14th May, 1977, 185–200. Amsterdam: John Benjamins.

Kahn, Daniel. 1980. Syllable-based generalizations in English phonology. New York: Garland Press.

Kaisse, Ellen M. and Patricia A. Shaw. 1985. On the theory of lexical phonology. In Colin J. Ewen and John M. Anderson (eds.), Phonology yearbook 2, 1–30, Cambridge: Cambridge University Press.

Kaye, Jonathan D. 1982. Harmony processes in Vata. In Harry van der Hulst and Norvil Smith (eds.), Structure of phonological representations 2, 385–452. Dordrecht: Foris.

———— and Jean Lowenstamm. 1981. Syllable structure and markedness theory. In A. Belletti, L. Brandi, and L. Rizzi (eds.), Theory of markedness in generative grammar. Proceedings of the GLOW Conference, 1979, 469–79. Pisa: Scuola Normale Superiore di Pisa.

Kiparsky, Paul. 1982. From cyclic phonology to lexical phonology. In Harry van der Hulst and Norvil Smith (eds.), Structure of phonological representations 1, 131–76. Dordrecht: Foris.

Kisseberth, Charles. 1984. Digo tonology. In George N. Clements and John Goldsmith (eds.), Autosegmental studies in Bantu tone, 105–182. Dordrecht: Foris.

Kohnen, B. 1933. Shilluk grammar. Verona: The Nigrizia School Press.

Kurłowicz, J. 1971. A problem of Germanic alliteration. In M. Barahmen, S. Helsztyński, and J. Kryanowski (eds.), Studies in language and literature in honour of Margaret Schlauch, 195–201. New York: Russell and Russell.

Laughren, Mary. 1984. Tone in Zulu nouns. In George N. Clements and John Goldsmith (eds.), Autosegmental studies in Bantu tone, 183–234, Dordrecht: Foris.

Leben, William R. 1971, Suprasegmental and segmental representation of tone. Studies in African Linguistics, Supp. 2:183–200.

———. 1973. Suprasegmental phonology. Bloomington: Indiana University Linguistics Club.

———. 1978. The representation of tone. In Victoria Fromkin (ed.), Tone: A linguistic survey, 177–220. New York: Academic Press.

———. 1980. Suprasegmental phonology. New York: Garland Press.

Levin, Juliette 1983. Reduplication and prosodic structure. Cambridge: MIT. ms.

Lindau, Mona. 1974. The feature advanced tongue root. In Erhard Voeltz (ed.), The 3rd annual conference on African linguistics, April, 1972, 127–33. Bloomington: Indiana University.

———. 1979. The feature expanded. Journal of Phonetics 7:163–76.

Lyons, John. 1971. Introduction to theoretical linguistics. Cambridge: Cambridge University Press.

McCarthy, John. 1981. A prosodic theory of nonconcatenative morphology. Linguistic Inquiry 12:373–418.

———. 1982. Prosodic templates, morphemic templates, and morphemic tiers. In Harry van der Hulst and Norvil Smith (eds.), Structure of phonological representations 1, 191–224. Dordrecht: Foris.

———. 1983. A prosodic account of Arabic broken plurals. Current Approaches in African Languages and Linguistics 1:289–320. Dordrecht: Foris.

———. 1986. ocp effects: Gemination and antigemination. Linguistic Inquiry, 17:207–63.

Michaels, David. 1987. Syllable structure, rules and principles. In XIV International congress of linguists (Comité International Permanent des Linguistes), 10–15, August, 1987. Berlin.

Mohanan, Karuvannur P. 1982. Lexical phonology. Bloomington: Indiana University Linguistics Club.

———. 1985. Syllable structure and lexical strata in English. In Colin J. Ewen and John M. Anderson (eds.), Phonology yearbook 2, 139–55. Cambridge: Cambridge University Press.

———. 1986. The theory of lexical phonology. Dordrecht: Reidel.

New International Version (NIV), Holy Bible. New York Bible Society. Sevenoak, Kent: Hodder and Stoughton Ltd.

Noske, Roland. 1982. Syllabification in French. In Harry van der Hulst and Norvil Smith (eds.), Structure of phonological representations 2, 257–310, Dordrecht: Foris.

———. 1987. Directional, lexical and postlexical syllabification and vowel deletion. In Proceedings of the XIth international congress of phonetic sciences 2. Tallinn: Academy of Sciences of the Estonian SSR.

Shilluk Phonology   209

Okoth-Okombo, Duncan. 1982. Dholuo morphophonemics in a generative framework. V. Heine, W. J. G. Mohlig and Franz Rottland (eds.). Berlin: Deitrich Reimer Verlag. Supp. 2.

Persson, Andrew. 1984. The relationship of the languages of the Sudan. In Richard Watson and Wanda Pace (eds.), Occasional papers in the study of Sudanese languages 3:1–6. Juba, Sudan: Summer Institute of Linguistics and the Institute for Regional Languages.

Pesetsky, D. 1979. Russian morphology and lexical theory. MIT. ms.

Pike, Kenneth L. 1947. Phonemics. Ann Arbor: University of Michigan Press.

Poser, William J. 1982. Phonological representations and action-at-a-glance. In Harry van der Hulst and Norvil Smith (eds.), Structure of phonological representations 2, 121–58. Dordrecht: Foris.

Pulleyblank, Douglas. 1983. Tone in lexical phonology. Ph.D. dissertation, MIT, Cambridge, Massachusetts.

———. 1986. Tone in lexical phonology. Dordrecht: Reidel.

Reh, Mechthild. 1986. Classification of vowel phonemes in Anywak. Afrikanistische Arbeitspapiere 7, Schriftenreihe des Kolner Instituts fur Afrikanistik, 5–32.

The Rejaf Language Conference. 1928. Chaired by J. G. Matthew, O.B.E. Rejaf, Sudan.

Rubach, Jerzy. 1985. Lexical phonology: Lexical and postlexical derivations. In Colin J. Ewen and John M. Anderson (eds.), Phonology yearbook 2, 157–72. Cambridge: Cambridge University Press.

Schane, Sanford A. 1973. Generative phonology. Englewood Cliffs, New Jersey: Prentice-Hall.

Schuh, Russell G. 1978. Tone rules. In Victoria Fromkin (ed.), Tone: A linguistic survey, 221–56. New York: Academic Press.

Selkirk, Elizabeth. 1982. The syllable. In Harry van der Hulst and Norvil Smith (eds.), Structure of phonological representations 2, 337–84. Dordrecht: Foris.

Siegel, Dorothy. 1979. Topics in English morphology. New York: Garland Press.

Sommerstein, Alan H. 1977. Modern phonology. London: Edward Arnold.

Tucker, Archibald N. 1955. The verb in Shilluk. Mitt. des Instituts fur Orientforschung, 421–62.

——— and Margaret A. Bryan. 1966. Linguistic analyses of the non-Bantu languages of East Africa. London: Oxford University Press.

Vago, Robert M., ed. 1980. Issues in vowel harmony. Proceedings of the Cuny linguistics conference on vowel harmony, 14 May, 1977. Amsterdam: John Benjamins.

van der Hulst, Harry. 1985a. The framework of nonlinear generative phonology. In Harry van der Hulst and Norvil Smith (eds.), Advances in nonlinear phonology, 3–58. Dordrecht: Foris.

——. 1985b. Vowel harmony in Hungarian: A comparison of segmental and autosegmental anaylses. In Harry van der Hulst and Norvil Smith (eds.), Advances in nonlinear phonology, 267–303. Dordrecht: Foris.

—— and Norvil Smith, eds. 1982. The structure of phonological representations 1 and 2. Dordrecht: Foris.

—— and ——, eds. 1985. Advances in nonlinear phonology. Dordrecht: Foris.

Voeltz, Erhard, ed. 1974. The third annual conference on African linguistics, April, 1972. Bloomington: Indiana University.

Watson, Richard and Wanda Pace, eds. 1984. Occasional papers in the study of Sudanese languages 3. Juba, Sudan: Summer Institute of Linguistics and the Institute for Regional Languages.

Wise, Mary Ruth and Richard Watson. 1985. Occasional papers in the study of Sudanese languages 4. Juba, Sudan: Summer Institute of Linguistics and the Institute for Regional Languages.

Westermann, Diedrich. 1912. The Shilluk people. Glückstadt: J. J. Augustin.

Index

A

applicative 66, 80
association convention 15, 154, 156, 159, 163, 174, 185
association lines 9, 14–15, 60, 154
autosegment 11–14, 54, 60–61, 145, 154, 176
autosegmental phonology 9

B

benefactive 68, 74, 80, 138, 140–42, 145, 153
bracket erasure 6, 169

C

collective (COLL) 64, 109, 124–27, 130, 146, 167, 182
complement 68–69, 71–76, 96, 138, 142, 175
complement rule(s) 16, 33–34, 96, 175
compound words 46, 63, 77–78, 163
consonant alternation 142, 177
consonant harmony 11, 153, 173, 180
constituent order 69–72

D

default rules 17, 33–34, 189
downdrift 44, 50
downstep 44, 48–49, 192

E

epenthesis 6–7, 17, 33–34
expanded pharynx 19, 23, 28, 173

F

feature(s) 14–15, 29–32, 83, 94, 100, 200
Form A 68, 74–76, 80, 82–88, 94, 109–10, 118, 136–38, 142, 146, 156, 178, 190, 203
Form B 68, 74–76, 79–80, 82–84, 87–88, 94, 109–10, 118, 136–42, 145–46, 156, 178, 190, 203
fortis 22, 26–27, 37–40, 42, 200

G

geminates 26–27, 37–39, 42, 83, 115, 117–18, 120, 124, 126–30, 133, 135–37, 143–44, 183, 190, 200, 203
generative phonology 3–4, 11, 16, 29, 189
glides 24–25, 30, 36, 42, 84–85, 102, 105

H

harmony 11–12, 18, 153, 172–73, 175, 177, 180

I

inflection 63–64, 109, 113, 115, 121, 133, 154, 161, 164, 167, 176–77, 181–83, 191–92
instrument 68, 74, 142–45, 153

L

length 3–4, 26–28, 38–39, 43, 77, 83, 97, 109, 140, 142, 161, 191
lexical item 6, 81, 84–85, 92, 172
lexical phonology 3–6, 8, 169, 189

211

lexicon 5, 8, 18, 31, 84–85, 91, 96–97, 153, 157, 159–60, 163, 169–70, 172, 189, 192

M

mapping 15, 154, 156, 164
metathesis 130, 132
morpheme 7–8, 10, 49, 58, 84, 89, 91–92, 126, 142, 153–56, 161–62, 164, 183–86, 189–90
morphotonemics 163

N

nasal assimilation 183
nasalization 153, 167, 177, 182–84
non-complement (N-CMP) 73–74
nonlinear phonology 4–5, 9, 11
nouns 8, 27, 33, 47, 54, 56–58, 63–67, 77–81, 84, 86–89, 92, 97, 109, 124, 136, 139–40, 145–46, 153, 159, 162–63, 167, 169, 172, 182–86, 189–90

O

orthography 3–4, 202–3

P

passive 66–69, 71–72, 75–76, 79–80, 137–38
phoneme 3–4, 23–26, 28–31, 37, 94
phonetic inventory 21–22, 28
plosives 39–42, 83, 142, 182–83
plural (PL) 27, 34, 47, 52–59, 63–65, 79–81, 83–87, 89–91, 93–94, 97, 109, 123–24, 127–31, 133–40, 145–46, 154–55, 162, 170–72, 182–83, 185, 189–90
postlexical module 7
prefix 45–46, 51–52, 57–58, 63, 77–79, 81, 96, 156, 158, 160–63, 173–75, 177, 191–92

Q

qualitative 66–67, 73, 80

R

redundancy rules 4, 16–17, 32–33, 60
resyllabification (RESYLL) 114, 116–17, 121, 128, 134–35, 144–45, 168, 170–72
rime 10, 100–101, 104–10
root 7–8, 26, 34–36, 40, 45–46, 51–52, 55, 57–58, 64, 72–74, 77, 79, 81–86, 89, 93–94, 96–97, 109, 111, 117, 122, 129–33, 136, 140–42, 144, 155–57, 159–63, 166–67, 169, 172–82, 185, 190–92, 196
Rules
    Branching Coda Constraint (BCC) 108, 124, 148, 195
    Coda Syllabification Principle (CSP) 42, 106–12, 117, 120, 124, 127, 133–36, 138–44, 149, 166, 168, 171–72, 187, 197
    Complement Rule 32–34, 175–177, 181, 187–88, 200
    Deletion Rule 165, 169, 171–72, 176, 187–88, 198
    Diphthong High Spreading Rule (DHSR) 42–43, 62, 202
    Dual Syllable Head Pruning Rule (DSHP) 107, 114–17, 121, 127, 133–34, 136, 139–43, 162, 164–65, 168–72, 177, 184, 187, 198
    Glide And Vowel Constraint (GVC) 37, 62, 106, 147, 193
    I-incorporation (IIP) 34, 130–33, 138–40, 145, 170–72, 187, 191
    Initial Consonant Sequence (ICS) 36, 62, 105, 146–47, 192–93
    Initial Consonant Sequence Constraint (ICSC) 36, 62, 105, 147, 192
    Initial Geminate Consonant Sequence Constraint (IGCSC) 41, 62, 106, 147, 193
    Intervocalic Aspiration Rule (IAR) 41–42, 62, 139, 201
    Marked Vowel Coda Constraint (MVCC) 119–20, 148, 196
    Marked Vowel Coda Delinking (MVCD) 120–21, 136, 150, 198

Shilluk Phonology 213

Nuclear Adjunction (NA) 131–32, 134, 140, 151, 171–72, 187, 199
Obligatory Contour Principle (OCP) 154, 161, 185
Off-glide High Spreading Rule (OHSR) 43, 62, 202
Phonetic Shortening Rule (PSR) 38, 42, 62, 201
Phonological Word Constraint (PWL) 114–16, 121, 127, 134, 148, 172, 196
Plural Metathesis Rule (PMR) 131, 150, 199
Possessive Nasal Attachment (PNA) 184–187, 197
Possessive Tone Assignment (PTA) 162–63, 172, 185–86, 196
Referential Determiner Nasal Attachment (RDNA) 183–84, 186, 197
Root Association Rule (RAR) 158–64, 174–77, 181, 185, 196
Root Vowel Spreading Rule (RVSR) 132, 140, 151, 171, 187, 200
Root-final Consonant Delinking Rule (RFCDR) 144, 152, 200
Segment Delinking Convention (SDC) 109, 112, 117, 121, 125, 133–35, 138–45, 149, 166, 168, 171–72, 187, 195
Syllable Head Constraint (SHC) 106–7, 148, 194
Syllable Head Movement (SHM) 131, 140, 151, 170–72, 187, 199
Syllable-final Devoicing (SFD) 39–41, 62, 201
Tense-voicing Rule (TVR) 40, 42, 62, 201
Tensing Rule (TR) 37–38, 41–42, 62, 139, 201
Tone Association (TA) 156, 158, 194
Tone Deletion Rule (TDR) 165, 168–72, 187–88, 198
Tone Simplification Rule (TSR) 167–69, 172, 186, 196
Vocalic Association Constraint (VAC) 107, 149, 195
Vocalic Delinking (VD) 107, 116, 121, 128, 134–36, 141, 149, 165, 168, 169–70, 176, 195

Well-formedness Condition (WFC) 14, 54, 154, 192

S

semantic 54, 71, 81, 136, 162, 183, 185
singular (SG) 56–59, 63–65, 79–81, 83–87, 89–91, 93–94, 96, 121, 128, 135, 146, 153, 155, 162, 167, 182–86, 189–90
singulative (SGLT) 64, 79, 97, 109, 111, 113, 120, 124–27, 146
suffix 45–46, 48, 52, 58, 63–64, 79–80, 94, 96, 117, 130–33, 140, 142, 155–60, 162–64, 167, 169, 172–77, 184, 191–92
syllabification (SYLL) 10, 34, 42, 101–2, 104–9, 113–21, 124, 142–45, 148–50, 162, 164, 166, 168–72, 177, 184, 187, 194, 197–99, 201
syllable 9, 18, 27, 30, 32, 34, 39–40, 42–43, 45–48, 50, 52–58, 72, 77, 89, 92, 97, 99–102, 104–13, 122, 127–28, 137, 145–46, 154, 156, 158–60, 162, 166, 169–70, 172, 176–78, 191
onset 10, 40, 100–2, 104–5, 113

T

template 7, 102–4, 112, 122–23, 136, 194
tier 7, 39, 54–55, 60–61, 92, 95, 136, 154–56, 161, 164, 176, 178, 189
CV 9, 13, 100, 156–57, 159, 178, 191
timing 15, 17, 85, 95, 136, 142, 154, 164
tone 44–61, 89–91, 95, 133, 153, 192
floating 133, 163–64
tone-bearing unit (TBU) 49, 53, 55, 60–61, 154, 156–57, 163

U

underlying representation 4, 10, 18, 32, 47, 81, 83–86, 88–89, 92, 96–97, 102, 116, 118, 122–28, 136–38, 140–44, 146, 153–54, 175, 189–90
underspecification 3–5, 32, 59, 175, 189
theory 4, 15–17, 32, 175, 189

214   Index

underspecified 32–35, 59, 86, 128, 136,
    156, 158, 175–76, 180–82, 192

V

verbs 3, 8, 63, 66–67, 71–76, 79–81, 83–
    89, 92–94, 109, 131, 136–40, 145,
    153, 189, 202
  intransitive 66–67, 71–74, 76, 79
  transitive 66–68, 71–74, 76, 79, 85,
    189–90
vowel
  alternatingly short and long 109, 111,
    113, 116, 118, 120, 128, 132, 135–
    39, 146, 191
  breathiness 3, 28
  harmony 11, 173–77
  height 83, 88–89, 95
  invariably long 18, 109, 117–20, 122,
    133, 135–36, 146, 191
  invariably short 18, 109–11, 113, 128,
    135–36, 139, 146, 191
  length 3–4, 24, 29, 39, 43, 123, 191
  zero alternation 85

CPSIA information can be obtained
at www.ICGtesting.com
Printed in the USA
LVHW010728140622
721221LV00008B/675